SEATTLE'S *best-kept* SECRET

SEATTLE'S *best-kept* SECRET

A History of the Lighthouse for the Blind, Inc.

Celebrating Ninety Years

Junius Rochester

ISBN 0-9648950-3-x

With special support from

2501 South Plum Street
Seattle, Washington 98114

Designed by Laura Clark
Seattle, Washington

Printed in Canada

*Cover Images taken from photographs
of brooms and canteen caps.*

To EMPLOYEES & VOLUNTEERS
Past, Present and Future
The Heart and Soul of
The Lighthouse for the Blind, Inc.

TABLE OF CONTENTS

Love looks not with the eyes, but with the mind,
And therefore is wing'd Cupid painted blind.

—William Shakespeare, 1595
A Midsummer Night's Dream

FOREWORD

Following are two statements by true friends of the Seattle Lighthouse. Ray Haman's foreword encompasses the observations of a longtime board member and supporter—someone who has more than forty years of experience with the intricacies of this complex nonprofit agency.

Alan Mullaly's foreword comments on the fifty-year relationship between the Lighthouse and Boeing—the perspective of the organization's oldest and strongest community partner.

The Seattle Lighthouse for the Blind, Inc., is pleased and honored to have these gentlemen welcome readers to our ninety-year history.

> George Jacobson, President
> The Lighthouse for the Blind, Inc.
> Seattle, Washington

The book you are about to read is not just a history of a venerable Seattle institution and its ninety-year struggle to provide visually impaired individuals with effective training and meaningful employment. It is also a story of evolving attitudes and expanding opportunities—evolving attitudes toward visually impaired individuals and their capabilities, and expanding opportunities for them to become self-sufficient in their careers and private lives.

In the beginning, those who sought to train and employ blind and partially sighted individuals focused on labor-intensive work such as caning chairs, winding brooms, and weaving cloth. Only after World War II did the Washington State Rehabilitation and Training Center for the Blind and its marketing arm, a nonprofit corporation called Handcrest, begin to train and employ legally blind workers to operate a machine shop producing metal parts for Boeing aircraft. This modest beginning as a Boeing supplier resulted in a change in attitude concerning the capabilities of Handcrest employees and a dramatic expansion of their employment opportunities. The Seattle Lighthouse continues to be a Boeing supplier, and the importance of The Boeing Company in revealing the capabilities of the Lighthouse workforce cannot be overstated.

I was asked to write this foreword because I served for several years on the governing board of Handcrest until its merger with the Lighthouse in 1964; and I have been a member of the board of trustees of the Lighthouse continuously since 1962. Having personally participated in the governance of this enterprise, and having observed its talented management and employees for more than half of its history, I have witnessed firsthand the evolving attitudes and expanding opportunities that Junius Rochester, the author of this book, explores in the following pages.

The author also notes the dramatic change in governance of the Seattle Lighthouse that occurred following the merger with Handcrest. Until 1964 the board of trustees of the Lighthouse was composed almost exclusively of women, most of whom were married to members of the Seattle business establishment. The late Kay (Mrs. Robert Denny) Watt once described these women as "Ladies Bountiful." (That term would not be considered politically correct today, but those women cared more about their charitable cause than political correctness.)

By contrast, almost all Handcrest directors were men. Handcrest was formed to market goods produced by blind workers at the Washington State Rehabilitation and Training Center for the Blind, and most of the founders of Handcrest and their successors were businessmen experienced in manufacturing and marketing. Although ophthalmologists skilled in diagnosing and treating eye disease and others who have experienced eye disease personally or with family members have served on the governing boards of Handcrest and the Lighthouse, in recent years most Lighthouse board members have been business and professional men and women.

Not surprisingly, a governing board dominated by capitalists places heavy emphasis on the creation, preservation, and prudent employment of capital. This has been fortuitous; the shift from labor-intensive work to more highly mechanized production techniques has required substantial investments in increasingly more automated and computerized manufacturing equipment. It has been apparent to the Lighthouse management and governing board that the more automated the equipment, the more level the playing field becomes between visually impaired workers and their sighted counterparts. Thus, prudent and often bold investments of capital are necessary to expand opportunities for the Lighthouse's unique workforce.

A number of years ago, when the Lighthouse purchased several milling machines for about $30,000 apiece, and each machine employed one blind person per shift, I made a mental note that $30,000 of capital was needed to create a job for one person. Later, the board was asked to approve the acquisition and installation of highly automated machines to produce computer paper and hanging file folders for sale to the federal government, and we were told that each machine would cost about $600,000 and employ six blind workers per shift. I then increased my estimate of the cost of job creation to $100,000 per worker. Actually, my estimates were low, because they did not include the cost of land and buildings to house the new machines and related inventories of raw material and finished products.

The cost of job creation continues to increase. Many newer machines are run by computers equipped with adaptive technology to make them accessible to visually impaired workers, but an enterprise devoted to expanding opportunities for its workforce must be prepared to employ the necessary capital. One challenge for the management and trustees of the Lighthouse is to assure that the capital will be there when needed. Another challenge is to develop new or expanded markets to keep pace with increased productivity. Actually, spending on capital equipment and facilities goes hand in hand with marketing, and usually the market for a new product is identified before new equipment is acquired to manufacture the product.

As the author notes in Chapter 7, "On Hood Canal," not all Lighthouse programs create revenue. One of these is the annual Deaf-Blind Retreat, now in its twenty-sixth year. The Seattle Lighthouse is proud of its pioneering efforts to provide services for Deaf-Blind individuals, including training and employment. Visitors who tour the Lighthouse facilities in Seattle will see Deaf-Blind individuals and their sighted interpreters communicating by using American Sign Language and its tactile version. Communication is made possible by four arms and four hands and twenty fingers moving at lightning speed. I have seen this phenomenon many times, yet I am still amazed by the technique. Both the Deaf-Blind individuals and their interpreters possess skills that are beyond my comprehension. If you visit the Lighthouse Web site (www.seattlelighthouse.org), you will be impressed, and you will be more impressed to learn that the Web site designer is a Lighthouse Deaf-Blind supervisory employee. See what I mean by evolving attitudes and expanding opportunities?

All of us who serve on the board of trustees have great admiration for the entire Lighthouse workforce, both the visually impaired and those who provide them with support services. We are also proud of the Lighthouse management team, which for more than forty years has been led by Rudy Elmer and his successor, George Jacobson. The success of the Seattle Lighthouse has been due to the skill and dedication of its employees.

Blindness will always be with us through disease, genetics, or accidents, but I predict that in the future the Seattle Lighthouse will still be there with even more innovative ways to level the playing field. The history of the struggle of two organizations—Handcrest and the Lighthouse—to expand opportunities for visually impaired people awaits you in the following pages. Then you are invited to increase your knowledge of these matters by taking a tour of the Lighthouse. I hope you will agree that it is "Seattle's best-kept secret."

Raymond W. Haman
Board Member

———

"No pessimist ever discovered the secrets of the stars, or sailed to an uncharted land, or opened a new heaven to the human spirit."

This quotation from Helen Keller epitomizes the parallel relationship that has existed between The Boeing Company and Seattle Lighthouse for many years. It was 1951 when employees at the Lighthouse for the Blind began building airplane parts for Boeing, and ever since, our ideals have intertwined on virtually every Boeing commercial jet.

Just think about that for a minute. Not long after we established a business relationship, Boeing expanded the elements of flight with the first jet-powered commercial airplane, the 707. As years progressed and Boeing followed with a succession of airplanes, the Lighthouse extended operations and built a community-service foundation that today remains linked to events that shape our lives.

Fundamentally, the Lighthouse helps connect people. It is a partner to Boeing, which helps connect people and economies of the world through flight. Lighthouse connects to our servicemen and -women, assembling and shipping canteens and water containers to the front lines of conflicts around the world. And through their dedication to providing manufacturing employment, the Lighthouse connects people with opportunities.

When you read this rich, compelling history of the Lighthouse, you will be taken on the journey of an agency that began operations by offering social and recreational activities. Over time, the Lighthouse grew into a vibrant employer that today continues to adapt to changing technology and business requirements.

The Lighthouse now is a sophisticated operation built by the desire to make its business as competitive as possible, producing quality work that meets the highest standards of its customers. By running a successful business, they create job opportunities that enable their employees to be self-sufficient and independent. This book shares wonderful, inspirational stories about the people of the Lighthouse and their intelligence, dedication, and passion to do great things. It also shares their phenomenal efforts and desire to conquer challenges that stand before them; to confront the improbable with confidence buoyed by positive thinking; to dare to dream of something better for our world, for our community, and for themselves.

I am personally very proud of our shared history and partnership. Boeing believes that the true quality of any company is measured not only by the integrity of its products and services, but also by the strength of its partnership with the larger community. Our half-century association with the Lighthouse is a shining example of that enduring commitment to the community.

The past 100 years of commercial aviation have clearly shown that by working together, we can accomplish difficult tasks many thought were impossible. Our partnership with the Lighthouse is based on mutual ideals, including the willingness to change, grow, and forever reach for new frontiers. It's also a partnership fostered by a shared yearning, as Helen Keller so aptly said, to "discover the secrets of the stars, or sail to an uncharted land, or open a new heaven to the human spirit."

> Alan Mulally
> President and CEO
> Boeing Commercial Airplanes

INTRODUCTION

"Things change" is a familiar story. Recognizing this truism, The Lighthouse for the Blind, Inc., in Seattle, Washington, has adjusted its products, programs, marketing approaches, and general outlook over the past ninety years.

The Lighthouse has occupied several Seattle locations. Other changes are occurring today. The Lighthouse history you hold in your hands is a recent example of this evolutionary process. One thing has not changed: providing employment and training and support services for people who are blind, Deaf-Blind, and blind with other disabilities.

Several years ago the Lighthouse board decided to raise the profile of the organization to inform a larger audience about Lighthouse activities and accomplishments. That decision involved several steps, such as producing an employee-named newsletter called *Horizons* and establishing a foundation (noted in detail at the end of this book). Other steps included developing appropriate mailing lists, hiring outstanding people to staff the new Public Relations and Resource Development Department, encouraging public tours of the Lighthouse, and writing a history of the organization. My appearance, as in-house writer and historian, occurred shortly thereafter—late 2003.

Telling this story was delightfully abetted by helpful staff, employees, and board members, and by digging through cartons of records, notes, and photographs. "Outside" information was found at the Central Branch of the Seattle Public Library, the Museum of History and Industry (MOHAI), the Washington State Jewish Historical Society, Boeing Company archives, and the Washington Talking Book and Braille Library. Perhaps the most rewarding sources—bits and pieces of Lighthouse fact and lore—came from personal interviews with Lighthouse board members, staff, supporters, and former employees.

In brief, the Seattle Lighthouse story began in 1914, with the formation of a social organization called the Seattle Association for the Blind. Blind people and their friends and family members at that time saw a need for coming together to discuss problems and issues relevant to their interests, and resolving matters of common concern. The association also stimulated a low-key "political" effort to attract the attention of local officials regarding education, transportation, employment, and economic matters related to blind persons. A larger question of education occasionally arose: i.e., informing the general public about prejudice toward and misunderstanding about blind people.

In 1916, several dedicated women helped the association find employment for blind people. One result was the establishment of a workshop at 1208 Fourth Avenue,

Seattle, on the present site of the Fairmont Olympic Hotel. This small commercial undertaking sold jigsaw puzzles and baskets made by blind and partially sighted workers.

Establishing the association and shop were victories. However, more was needed. The next step was the official April 1918 incorporation of The Lighthouse for the Blind, Inc., in Seattle, Washington. Leadership of that step came from a group of socially prominent women, a contingent that guided the Lighthouse for more than forty years. That remarkable story is told in the following pages.

In 1925, a Lighthouse building was constructed at 131 Elliott Avenue West, present site of the *Seattle Post-Intelligencer* newspaper. From that point forward, Lighthouse history moved through several phases: the making and selling of crafts (brooms, place mats, furniture caning, and other items), and introducing innovative education and training programs.

In 1964, a business (previously sponsored by the state) called Handcrest, Inc., merged with Seattle Lighthouse. In 1967, Seattle Lighthouse moved to its present location in Rainier Valley. Another large step was the introduction of training and meaningful jobs for Deaf-Blind persons (in 1969—the Lighthouse was among the first blindness agencies to do so in the nation). The first Deaf-Blind Lighthouse employees were Christine Gilbrough and two sisters, Lavena and Lillian Meske. This was followed by affiliation with the Helen Keller National Center and the in-house design and manufacture of parts and products for local companies and national defense. More recently, new technology has allowed blind, partially sighted, Deaf-Blind, and individuals with other disabilities to manufacture and market a range of products in competition with firms across the country.

Although I was familiar with the name "Lighthouse for the Blind" and had driven past its site on Martin Luther King Jr. Way numerous times (the address, however, is on nearby Plum Street), it was not until I visited the premises that the organization's nature and spirit became clear.

Like most Seattle-area residents, my experience with people who are blind and other individuals with disabilities had been minimal. However, my background includes a lifelong friendship with a blind college friend and his daughter. He was blinded by a farm accident and his daughter has retinitis pigmentosa (RP). Both are attorneys. Another close friend from high school days, and a current member of the Lighthouse board of trustees, has two sons with RP, one of whom is employed at tha Seattle Lighthouse.

Other "impressions" include my knowledge of the late Stephen B.L. Penrose's term as the (blind) president of my alma mater, Whitman College. Also, I am a fan of the late blind singer Ray Charles, who got his start in the Tacoma-Seattle area. I knew Pearl Wanamaker, Washington state senator and former longtime Washington State Superintendent of Public Instruction, and attended Whitman with her daughter. I later learned that Wanamaker had a keen interest in helping disabled students. She also played a role in the 1964 merger of Handcrest and Seattle Lighthouse.

Getting a close look at American Sign Language (ASL) was a new personal experience. It is a language of its own and I marvel at its users' dexterity, speed, and apparent accuracy. The only previous exposure I had to "signing" came from my research on the 1803–1806 Lewis and Clark expedition—we are now celebrating the bicentennial of that great adventure. ASL, of course, has no connection with Indian signing.

Issues and tales related to blind and Deaf-Blind individuals crop up in surprising places. For example, the late scientist/writer Stephen Jay Gould described an early major-league ballplayer, William "Dummy" Hoy, who was deaf, in his posthumously published book *Triumph and Tragedy in Mudville: A Lifelong Passion for Baseball* (W.W. Norton & Co., 2003). Under the section titled "Heroes Large, Small, and Fallen," Hoy is noted by Gould as one of the national pastime's cleverest players. Nationally known writer Ved Mehta describes building a new home in his book, *Building House and Home on an Enchanted Island* (Thunder's Mouth Press/Nation Books, 2003). Mehta claims that he pursued his construction project to "defy the accepted notion that the blind must keep to their pitiful place." In July 2003, I read that the United Parcel Service settled a discrimination lawsuit in which the company agreed to take steps to accommodate deaf workers. And so it goes, but these references usually attract little notice by non-disabled observers.

What can we say about the name "Lighthouse"? That moniker of course means a beacon—perhaps a bright light of help and hope, of accomplishment, of aspiration. Although most sources indicate that Lighthouse International in New York City is the oldest (1905—actually incorporated in 1906), the Chicago Lighthouse is celebrating its ninety-eighth birthday in 2004 and Cincinnati's Clovernook Center for the Blind now claims more than 100 years of accomplishment. Seattle's Lighthouse—if we include the forerunner Seattle Association for the Blind (1914)—will light ninety anniversary candles in 2004.

The term "sheltered workshop" is sometimes applied to organizations that provide a variety of services to disabled or partially disabled staff and workers. The term itself and the philosophy behind the phrase expose a divergence of opinion regarding assisting blind people and others with disabilities. Some believe that blind people and others should not be treated differently except for basic workplace accommodations, which are legal rights in America. Unfortunately, disabled Americans often have difficulty finding employment or face barriers in receiving accommodation and support to which they are entitled.

So-called "sheltered" activities offer specially developed facilities, training, staffing, and technology usually designed for—and sometimes by—disabled participants. Seattle Lighthouse is an agency specializing in the employment of people with disabilities.

Lighthouse employees want to live independent, self-sufficient lives, making their own choices and charting their own destinies. Many seek a safe, comfortable workplace and long-term employment. Over the years, as

Lighthouse manufacturing has increased and become more complicated, it must be said that the term "sheltered," when referring to Seattle Lighthouse, is no longer applicable.

One cannot embark on a local history project without seeing the larger picture. The Seattle Association for the Blind was founded the same year (1914) that "Miss Aunt Nellie" Cornish established her school of allied arts. (Cornish's name would appear in 1918 on the list of Lighthouse founders.) The Lake Washington Ship Canal opened in 1917, altering the waterfronts of Lake Washington and Lake Union. In 1918, the Frederick & Nelson department store opened in Seattle and the Great War (World War I) came to an end. Labor unrest, epitomized by activities of the Industrial Workers of the World ("Wobblies"), contributed to the Seattle General Strike of 1919. The nation then moved down a long, dry road called Prohibition.

Seattle in the 1930s was, like the rest of the country, in the throes of the Great Depression. "Hoovervilles"—like the tin and cardboard village that mushroomed near today's King Street railroad station—became part of the urban landscape. By the early 1940s, World War II dominated the national fabric. Defense industries surrounded Puget Sound, and food and gasoline rationing was in place. Despite these upheavals and inconveniences, Seattle Lighthouse continued to manufacture brooms, place mats, and other products.

During the uncertain 1950s, marked by Winston Churchill's "Iron Curtain" speech, the U.S. participated in the Korean conflict. This somber decade saw the Lighthouse distribute free white canes, make calls on shut-ins, arrange shopping trips for blind persons, and negotiate reduced transportation rates on railroads and bus lines for disabled persons.

The Lighthouse for the Blind story includes unique aspects. For example:

1. The Lighthouse has experienced almost a century of growth and change in the Pacific Northwest, from crafts to manufacturing, employing hundreds of people who in many cases might otherwise have been denied opportunities to contribute—a lost resource and undoubtedly involving personal tragedies.

2. It is proud to be among the first such organizations to hire Deaf-Blind workers, and is the nation's leader in employing, training, and supporting people who are Deaf-Blind.

3. The Lighthouse was an early organizer of internationally recognized camps—now called retreats—for Deaf-Blind people.

4. The Lighthouse has received a number of national awards, including the 1994 Fleet Industrial Center of Puget Sound "For . . . outstanding efforts in Providing the Opportunity for Disabled Workers to contribute to our [the fleet's] Mission." In 1995, the Defense Personnel Support Center gave the Lighthouse an award "In Recognition of the Outstanding Achievement, Superior Performance and Timely Delivery [of U.S. Defense products]. In 1998 Lighthouse received the National Industries for the Blind (NIB) Blind Achievement Award.

5. A stable staff—many boasting more than twenty-five years of experience—accomplishes product design, marketing assistance, and training for underutilized employees.
6. Lighthouse employees (263 at the end of fiscal year 2003; 282 as of March 2004) receive compensation based on fair market analysis. The Lighthouse's objectives have been to attract excellent employees, retain employees, reward employees for job performance, and remain fiscally responsible. Each year the Lighthouse reviews market data from the Puget Sound area to ensure pay practices that are consistent with the prevailing wage guidelines from the Department of Labor.

This overview/history of the Lighthouse can serve as an introduction to the lives and accomplishments of many disabled residents of Seattle and beyond, but the reader is invited to personally visit Lighthouse premises in Rainier Valley. That's where the real story can be found.

Junius Rochester
Seattle, Washington

CHAPTER 1
An Author's Primer

Looking at the Seattle Lighthouse in isolation gives an out-of-focus, skewed picture. Many events and heroes made contributions to the blind and partially sighted population.

In the Western world, the French took the lead in this field, with philosopher Denis Diderot's studies of blind people. Diderot wrote, "I found that of the senses the eye is the most superficial, the ear the most arrogant, smell the most voluptuous, taste the most superstitious and fickle, touch the most profound and philosophical."

Valentin Haüy took up Diderot's interests in this field in the 1780s. He was appalled to see people mocking and teasing blind citizens. Haüy picked a blind beggar—a boy named François Lesueur—as a subject. Haüy invented a slotted board into which wooden tiles were fitted. The upper surfaces were embossed with numbers or letters. When Lesueur ran his fingers over the embossed reverse side of the board he could identify them and thereby "read" simple sentences or series of numbers. Haüy's experiments may have been the first "books" for the blind.

Coincident with Haüy's work was the founding of France's first school for the deaf, by Abbé Charles-Michel de L'Epée, a priest. L'Epée is credited with modifying existing signs used by France's deaf population into a formal signing system. Students from throughout the region came to L'Epée's school, bringing their own homegrown versions of sign language. Daily personal interaction between L'Epée and his students evolved into a single, formalized language. Thus was born L'Epée's system of signs. As the founder of organized education for deaf people throughout the world, L'Epée eventually established twenty-one schools.

In 1821, Charles Barbier used a penknife to make puncture marks on paper, which he called "night writing." This invention allowed French soldiers to read battlefield messages in the dark and in silence. Its value was in its usefulness as a kind of code, not necessarily as a tool for the blind.

Our next hero left his name forever in the world of blind persons: Louis Braille. Braille had been blinded in an accident when he was three years old. As a student at a school for the blind, he learned to use his fingers to read Barbier's "dotted signs." His work in simplifying Barbier's code led to the first "alphabet" for blind people in 1832, known today as Braille.

More and different experiments were tried, but by the 1840s the Braille code was gaining popularity. It eventually spread to the United States and was accepted throughout the world by the 1930s. In the 1890s, Frank H. Hall, superintendent of the Illinois School for the Blind, invented a stereotype machine, the forerunner of Braille type-writers, allowing Braille to be reproduced more easily.

Currently there are four Braille codes: literary, music, Nemeth (mathematics), and computer Braille. Frederick K. Schroeder, writing in the *Journal of Visual Impairment & Blindness*, states, "[I]nnovative applications of Braille in the workplace are limited only by the creativity and imagination of the Braille user."

Braille offers literacy and broad possibilities of communication. It was commonly used in United States schools beginning in the 1940s. Dr. Walt Petersen has pointed out that children are natural learners of Braille. Today Braille is found beside written museum captions, in elevators, aboard modes of transportation, next to rest-room doorways, and in countless other locations. The road to achieving this important breakthrough for blind and partially sighted people has sometimes been slow and difficult.

The story of Helen Keller, who became deaf and blind as a child, is known by many, especially in America. Numerous books and plays have been written about Helen and her lifelong companion, Anne Sullivan, whom she referred to as "Teacher." Failure, suspicion, and fear were not foreign to Helen Keller. She grew up throwing tantrums and challenging everything and everyone she encountered.

Interacting with others has been a historic challenge for blind and Deaf-Blind individuals. That history has often been one of stigma, marginalization, and dominance by the hearing and seeing worlds.

Many Deaf-Blind people are members of the larger deaf community, which includes deaf, hard-of-hearing, Deaf-Blind, and hearing people such as family members and interpreters who interact socially or professionally with deaf people. Deaf individuals who share the language, history, and values of other deaf people identify themselves as culturally deaf (or deaf). On the fringes of this culture are those who are hard of hearing. Frequently, they do not want to be identified with a separate group or community.

American Sign Language (ASL) is a separate language from, say, English, Russian, and other languages, and is central to the deaf community.

Claire Blatchford, a deaf poet, tried to describe her world in a poem called "The Deaf Girl: A Memory:"

> Once as a child I heard Prokofiev
> On a record given to me.
> I played it all the afternoons,
> Wolves followed Peter through my rooms,
> Forests and snow lay about me.
> And then, as if to seal the spell,
> I woke one morning and could not tell
> Where in the silence of my room
> The wolves waited.
>
> The snow waited
> To melt. The forest did not stir.
> Peter had disappeared. Frozen
> In sunlight and shadows I've lived

With ears in my eyes, eyes in my heart.
Sometimes it seems that I have heard
Peter's footsteps in my heart-beat,
Sometimes I think I've seen
The wolves passing there.

Examples of the deaf and blind cultures are found in literature, film, drama, and fine arts. Sighted individuals and those without serious hearing limitations or other disabilities also appreciate these "different" experiences. Actor John Malkovich played a blind character in *Places in the Heart* (1984). Preparing for his role, Malkovich spent time in a Lighthouse for the Blind, learning to make cane chairs and brooms. A *Los Angeles Times* review described Malkovich's portrayal as that of an "intelligent, aloof and bitter man . . . without sentimentality." Blind characters struggled with life in Charlie Chaplin's *City Lights* (1931). Al Pacino's portrayal of the surly, angry, blind lieutenant colonel in *Scent of a Woman* (1992) was rewarded with an Oscar.

Author Martin Norden points out that before the 1970s stereotypical portrayals of people with physical disabilities in the theater and cinema fell into several categories: (1) heartwarming stories of courage and triumph; (2) violence-prone beasts; (3) comic characters; (4) saintly characters; (5) sweet young things emerging from miraculous cures.

Attitudes and opportunities for persons with disabilities in the United States began to change in the 1890s. In 1897, the Library of Congress provided services for the blind. By 1931, materials for the blind were produced and distributed to regional libraries by the Library of Congress. These meager beginnings started a quiet revolution.

Among Thomas Edison's more than 1,000 inventions were "phonograph books," which he said "speak to blind people." The first talking books included such works as the Bible, the Declaration of Independence, and Shakespeare's plays. The principle of talking books was later perfected with the invention of the 33 ⅓ rpm long-playing record. In 1935, Helen Keller worked with President Franklin D. Roosevelt's New Deal, notably the Works Progress Administration and the American Foundation for the Blind, to lobby Congress on behalf of the blind and visually impaired.

We all remember the 1960s, and its proliferation of tapes and cassettes, with today's digital process not far behind. At the Lighthouse, for example, state-of-the-art technology has been introduced as part of the workplace. In the year 2004, Lighthouse employees go home to operate a full range of life-changing adaptive technologies—like anyone else. Examples: talking microwaves; raised dots to indicate settings on stoves and washing machines.

W.W. Bauer, M.D., in a syndicated column in the *Seattle Post-Intelligencer* on March 22, 1954, attempted to summarize the condition of blind Americans. He implied that in most respects those with visual impairments had the same limitations and strengths as anyone else. He reckoned that there were 230,000 American blind citizens in

1954. They represented a cross section of all groups: "good, bad, busy, lazy, happy, grumpy, bright, stupid."

Most blind and partially sighted individuals, Dr. Bauer wrote, developed "compensatory keenness" over time. That is, they "trained" themselves—usually with help— to focus on their senses. There is nothing magical about this, he believed. Rather it is the result of conscious effort. He also pointed out that new skills must be "learned" by blind and partially sighted persons. That learning effort can be bolstered with outside help, such as the services offered by the Lighthouse. Among those bolstering steps, Bauer wrote, was the presence of courage and morale.

Besides the Seattle Lighthouse, its board of trustees, eminent physicians and psychologists, and an impressive cadre of volunteers and philanthropists, many Seattle- area public figures have shown a special interest in the blind and persons with other disabilities. One outstand- ing example was former *Post-Intelligencer* columnist Frank Lynch. During his time (1940s to 1960s) he wrote many columns about blindness and described individuals who were blind or partially sighted. His stories frequently mentioned The Lighthouse for the Blind, Inc.

Another *P.I.* reporter who got the facts right was Don Page. On December 10, 1964, Page wrote, "Already the image of The Lighthouse that Seattle has known since 1918 has almost disappeared. It no longer is simply a broomshop for the blind that sends out salesmen tapping from door to door with their wares. For better or worse, The Lighthouse is becoming an integrated industrial complex and social agency for the blind. Social workers are watching the transformation with interest. Organized labor is watching it with suspicion. The blind, themselves, are 'watching' the changes with mingled hope and apprehension."

What are the causes of blindness and vision impairment? Walter Petersen, M.D., who has practiced ophthalmology in Seattle for more than 45 years, and is past president of the Washington Academy of Eye Physicians and Surgeons, researched data on blindness and visual impairment. He prepared several brief papers on this subject, which are paraphrased below.

1. The World Health Organization (WHO) defines blindness as vision of 20/400 or less with best optical correction. In the United States legal blindness is 20/200—that is, what a person sees from 20 feet away contrasted with what a person with normal vision sees if standing 200 feet away. Visually impaired vision is defined as less than 20/40. Twenty-twenty (20/20) refers to the clarity with which a person views an object 20 feet away and is called normal vision.

2. There are three main treatable causes of blindness: cataracts, trachoma, and glaucoma (71 percent worldwide). Vitamin A deficiency is the most common cause of blindness in Africa. As the population ages, the incidence of bilateral (both eyes) blindness increases—principally from age-related macular degeneration (ARMD). Diabetes is a leading cause of blindness in the developed world, and injuries account for a smaller percentage of blindness worldwide.

3. The causes of blindness in the United States are difficult to estimate, largely because there is no national registry of blind people. Sixteen states have registries, but in those cases it is not always clear who does the registering, and no penalties exist for inaccuracy. According to Dr. Petersen, "in the future, the most common causes of blindness and vision difficulty in the U.S. will be ARMD and diabetic retinopathy."

4. Retinitis pigmentosa (RP), a group of hereditary retinal diseases, is often mentioned in Lighthouse literature. Dr. Petersen's sources estimate that there are 50,000 to 100,000 cases of RP in the U.S. The only treatment for RP is a daily dosage of 15,000 units of vitamin A, which may slow the progression of the disease but does not restore vision.

5. Usher syndrome is another familiar term at The Lighthouse for the Blind, Inc. This inherited disorder is characterized by hearing loss and a progressive loss of vision due to RP. There is no effective treatment. The Lighthouse has responded to the needs of people with this condition by introducing programs for Deaf-Blind people, including education and career guidance, teaching daily living skills, and annual retreats on beautiful Hood Canal in Washington state.

The Americans with Disabilities Act of 1990 (ADA) took effect on July 26, 1992. It is the law of the land and prohibits private and public employers from discriminating against qualified individuals with disabilities in job-application procedures, hiring, firing, advancement, compensation, and job training. It also defines "disability" and requires employers to "make an accommodation" to the known disability of a qualified applicant or employee. The Lighthouse for the Blind has provided such accommodations for decades—long before passage of the ADA. Despite the act's intentions, seven out of ten blind adults are not in the workforce. Those numbers have not changed appreciably since the ADA was enacted.

In the early 1970s, the Lighthouse began a pre-vocational training program for blind people with developmental disabilities. During this time, individuals living in institutions for the developmentally disabled could be placed into community-living "group homes" only if they had day-work experience. The Lighthouse, at the request of Washington State Services for the Blind, provided the needed jobs and training. These new services for multi-disabled blind people permanently changed the face of The Seattle Lighthouse for the Blind.

The above influences have touched the lives of many people. The Seattle Lighthouse welcomes the opportunity to expand readers' knowledge about this subject. Please contact them for a Lighthouse tour or literature.

People with physical or mental disabilities live on virtually every block of our communities. Attempting to understand their efforts to seek happy and productive lives is our common responsibility.

John Donne put it another way: "No man is an island, entire of itself; every man is a piece of the continent, a part of the main . . . any man's death diminishes me, because I am involved in mankind; and therefore never send to know for whom the bell tolls; it tolls for thee."

CHAPTER 2
Seattle Genesis

The Seattle Lighthouse grew from diverse local and national root systems.

Office holders in Washington's territorial and early statehood days tentatively and sporadically addressed the problems of disabled citizens. Following World War I, an influx of shipyard workers arrived in the Seattle area. Some of those immigrants and their family members were blind or otherwise disabled.

Puget Sound and its Queen City have frequently been the end of the line for pioneers seeking a new life in the West, and blind and Deaf-Blind residents still find the Pacific Northwest an ideal home. Moreover, in recent years, employment and training opportunities at the Seattle Lighthouse, including its unique Deaf-Blind Retreat now held on the shores of Hood Canal, attract individuals from around the world.

Perhaps the earliest indirect connections to the Lighthouse mandate can be traced to 1861. In that year Washington Territorial Secretary L. Jay S. Turney admonished the Legislature to enact measures to help those with physical or mental "handicaps." In Turney's words, "As enlightened men, and Christian legislators, you should make a suitable provision for unfortunate fellow beings, either deaf or dumb, blind, idiotic or insane. Such provisions for such unfortunates would gladden the hearts of all true philanthropists, and be hailed as an omen of that true and genuine religion which 'boasteth not itself.' " (Turney, accused of being a drunkard, held office for one year. He was dismissed in 1862.)

In 1881 the Territorial House of Representatives introduced but defeated an act to exempt blind persons from school tax. In November of the same year a bill was passed calling for the appropriation of $950 to send "deaf-mutes" of Washington Territory to the Oregon School for the Deaf. In 1885, Territorial Governor Watson C. Squire asked the Legislative Assembly to provide a local school for "handicapped" children. The result was the opening of the Washington School for Defective Youth at Vancouver, in Washington Territory, in 1886. That year the Territorial Legislature also enacted measures to provide for those with physical and mental disabilities, again using the expression "handicapped." (Seattle Lighthouse staff members point out that an inability to hear is not considered a "handicap" by those who use American Sign Language.)

The new school, with a five-member board of trustees and a director, was free to all "resident youth of Washington Territory." The board was required to include one "practical educator," one "physician," and one "lawyer." Qualifications for the director were strict: "a hearing man [not a woman] of sound learning and morals, not under 30 or more than 70 years of age." He was required to reside in the school. His free furnished quarters included "heat, light, and food." The director's compensation was $900 for the first year of his service, with a yearly increase up to $1,500.

The school started cautiously and on a small scale. A class of "deaf-mute" children in Tacoma, taught by Presbyterian minister W.D. McFarland, was adopted as the school's nucleus. The first home of the school was an abandoned hotel in downtown Vancouver. Local citizens showed their approval of the new institution by donating a 100-acre farm as part of the school's new home.

When the school's board lobbied the Territorial Legislature, it included the warning, in words typical of that era, that "deaf-mute and feeble-minded" children might be a threat to society, and ". . . if [those children are] permitted to grow up as ignorant animals, [they] will become an especially dangerous element in our population. With human powers for evil, they have no means of learning nearly all that elevates manhood above the brute creation." The board specified that the way to help these children was "the queen of all virtues, Charity!"

Today's Washington State School for the Blind is, of course, a different place than that of yesteryear. Charity remains an important virtue, but the professional atmosphere, staff, and support systems of the Vancouver school—like those of the Seattle Lighthouse—are far removed from the paternal attitudes, well-meaning as they may have been, of Washington's territorial days. And, to cite a Seattle connection, many Lighthouse employees attended the Washington State School for the Blind, which provides classes from kindergarten through 12th grade.

Activities pertaining to the disabled were occurring in Seattle during the Great War. At an unknown date an informal, unincorporated organization called the Seattle Association for the Blind was formed. Primarily social in nature, it led to an important move by the Charities Endorsement Committee of the Seattle Chamber of Commerce in 1914. Establishing a "shop for the blind" was the chamber's goal. On July 15, 1914, an ad hoc group called the Charity Organization Society issued a "Report on the Blind." Its findings were based on detailed information about sixty-two local blind people. The report classified them in this way: "One Good Eye (1); Deaf (4); Child—under seven years (1); Unknown Addresses (8); In (King) County Hospital—ages given and one individual labeled 'colored' (13); Living Outside of the City (9); Living in the City (26)."

The Chamber of Commerce report noted that few of the county hospital inmates would be able to take advantage of a shop for the blind. Others were "too old and feeble" or "suffer from paralysis or some other ailment in addition to blindness." It was also stated that seventeen of the blind were self-supporting or had independent means, while another nine were dependent on relatives or friends. The report claimed that a total of thirteen persons were "physically and mentally capable" of running or working in a shop and had expressed interest in such a project.

Incorporation of the Seattle Association for the Blind, on October 26, 1914, provided legal authority to run a shop. Incorporation gave the association the power to "advance the general welfare of the blind generally." Five men wrote and had notarized the articles of incorporation. They were W. Roy Clark, John Austin, John McLaughlin, Frederick Bentley, and John P. Hartman, who served as attorney for the association. Clark, Austin, and McLaughlin, a majority of the group, were blind— an impressive fact in those early years of the century. It was estimated at the time that there were nearly 100 blind people in the city of Seattle.

The new organization had specific purposes: " . . . [to] provide industries, employment, or plans for making the blind self-sustaining[;] . . . acquire . . . real and personal property, and use the same for the purposes of this corporation[;] borrow money when deemed necessary . . . [and] pledge by mortgage or otherwise the property of the corporation[; and] . . . carry on such business or otherwise act as may be conducive to the interest, welfare, and pecuniary advantage of the members thereof." Setting up and operating the shop was the next step. It was always the founders' goal to make the shop self-supporting.

In 1914, on headed stationery reading "Seattle Association for the Blind, Seattle, Washington," attorney John P. Hartman signed a letter to new parents requesting financial support for the association. Hartman's text offered congratulations to the parents and included a "lucky penny" for their newborn.

Two years later, on November 13, 1916, the association's bylaws were amended. Officer positions were out-lined, reports and minutes were required, a board of trustees was established, methods of handling funds were described, and committees were formed. Article III dealt with types of memberships: sustaining ($1), honorary ($50), and life ($200). In 1919, more than ninety people were listed as members of the association.

A "sheltered shop" was established in 1916 at 1208 Fourth Avenue, on the present site of Seattle's Fairmont Olympic Hotel. Credit for that operation is given to John P. Hartman and Harriet Kerlin Bentley—the first woman in a Lighthouse, or pre-Lighthouse, leadership position. Employment was restricted to blind and partially sighted individuals. The products of this small enterprise consist-ed of handmade jigsaw puzzles and baskets.

Seattle women now entered the picture in larger num-bers. Harriet Bentley, president, and Jennie Christopher, secretary, signed an amendment to the association's arti-cles of incorporation on January 8, 1917. The amend-ment to Article V allowed the board to expand from five members to fifteen. This was a turning point. An expand-ed board membership meant more involvement by women. From that point in time, and for the next forty years, eminent Seattle matrons (for more information, see Chapter 3) managed the association's affairs, including some of its later life as The Lighthouse for the Blind.

The name "Lighthouse" was known in other regions of the country. In 1918, that name was chosen for a revived version of the Seattle Association. On April 2, 1918, articles of incorporation for The Lighthouse for the

Blind, Inc., were signed at a gathering of socially and culturally prominent women. The signatories were as follows:

Virginia R. Soliday	*Ella D. Godwin*
Nellie C. Cornish	*Rose M. Greenstreet*
Kate McGraw Baxter	*Armeni T. Lawson*
Julia A. Ballinger	*Ellen R. Bacon*
Maude W. Fox	*Anne S. Delafield Dovey*
Mrs. M. A. Norton	*Harriet Kerlin Bentley*
Maude F. Schoenfeld	*Isabel B. Haines*
Evelyn Taylor	*Frances R. McLoughlin*
Mary Sanders	*Maude M. Bigelow*
Susie W. Smith	*Avis I. Markoe*
Mildred Whitcomb	*Elizabeth R. Brinkley*
Ethel Garrett Eddy	*Drusilla S. Percival*
Alice DeWitt Weston Ward	

The founders noted that they were "residents of the City of Seattle and citizens of the United States of America." It was also proclaimed that "women and/or men" could be "admitted" to the corporation, provided they were of "good moral character, . . . [and] can conscientiously subscribe to all the objects of [the] corporation." Selection of members would be made "without any reference whatever to or restriction upon their religious or political belief or profession."

Several features of this document are surprising. Article II is, in fact, a progressive statement for the year 1918. Emphasizing no reference or restriction relating to political, professional, or religious background seems more in tune with laws passed in the 1960s and later. It's also note-worthy that only one woman used the title "Mrs."; the other founders signed their first and last names.

The Seattle Lighthouse's founding names include representatives of Seattle's arts community, the wealthy class, professional interests, and pioneer families. Among the signers was Nellie C. Cornish, who founded the Seattle school for the performing and fine arts that bears her name. She does not mention the Lighthouse in her autobiography (*Miss Aunt Nellie*). Maude F. Schoenfeld was part of a family that ran a successful local furniture business. Julia A. Ballinger's husband, Richard, was a prominent attorney, former Seattle mayor, and U.S. Secretary of the Interior. Ethel Garrett Eddy was the wife of John W. Eddy, principal in the Skinner & Eddy Corporation, which dominated Puget Sound and Alaska shipping for many years. Mrs. Norton was the wife of William J. Norton, who ran a famous cafeteria on Second Avenue. The name Haines has roots in the Seattle law fraternity. Brinkleys have been active in Seattle affairs since the early 1900s, and Elizabeth Brinkley's husband, Robert Campbell Brinkley, was associated with the early Stone & Webster trolley car interests.

Article IV and its 13 subsections describe the "objects for which [the] corporation is formed." They might be summarized by the sentence: "To found, build, equip and/or maintain workshops, homes, asylums or other necessary provisions in caring for, assisting and making more useful the blind of the County of King, in the State of Washington, and others residing elsewhere . . ."

The Lighthouse for the Blind, Inc., now officially existed. It needed more space in which a "workshop" could be reestablished. As a result, a building on Fifteenth Avenue West was rented to accommodate basket weaving and chair caning.

A new product was introduced in this rented space that would be associated with the Lighthouse for many years—brooms. It should be pointed out that broom making ceased in about 1972, but even today Seattle residents identify the Lighthouse with that product. Because partially sighted or blind salespeople sold the brooms door to door, and few Seattle homes lacked a Lighthouse broom, that imprint has not faded. Broom making as a symbol of yesteryear, however, remains a proud step in the growth of Lighthouse activities and services.

*Making brooms at Lighthouse's Elliott Avenue
West location (1920s)*

Marketing Lighthouse products and finding outlets for brooms and other products of both the Lighthouse and Handcrest was a never-ending challenge. In June of 1963, the Lighthouse opened a Tacoma, Washington, distribution center at 917 South Thirty-eighth Street. Later that year, Associated Blind Products opened a shop at 1822 Broadway, in Seattle. Articles sold in the Broadway shop were made exclusively by blind people.

About the same time (1919) that the Seattle Lighthouse emerged, the Seattle Public Library established its Blind Division. The library wrote to approximately 1,000 blind people in Washington state and invited each of them to borrow books. Simultaneously, volunteers stepped forward to transcribe books into Braille and read to blind users at the Central Library. The Blind Division would survive as the Washington Talking Book and Braille Library in Seattle.

CHAPTER 3
Matrons & Clubs

Matron: "A married woman usu. marked by dignified maturity or social distinction" (Merriam-Webster's Collegiate Dictionary, Eleventh Edition).

Never underestimate the enthusiasm or influence of prominent families. Their social activities and affluent styles rarely interfere with tasks at hand. The women of the early Lighthouse board of trustees—most of whom were well connected—took their duties seriously and reached in all directions to find support. The Seattle Lighthouse's outstanding reputation grew to national, even international, proportions while being carefully watched by the board. The result was a busy, ever-evolving organization that accomplished many things.

By 1925, C.D. Stimson, a disabled entrepreneur (he had one arm), had established sawmills in the Ballard district, which was then a northern boundary of Seattle. Around the same time he initiated development of The Highlands, an exclusive residential district north of Seattle. In fact, real estate became a second and burgeoning source of Stimson family income.

In 1925, Stimson Mill Company donated a piece of surplus property at 131 Elliott Avenue West to the Lighthouse.

Making brooms at Lighthouse's Elliott Avenue West location, sometime after 1926

The exact arrangements are difficult to trace, but there is little doubt that eminent members of the Lighthouse board played roles in effecting this transfer. Building materials and labor, most of it from Stimson companies, resulted in the erection of a two-story frame building on the site. One room became the broom factory; the other housed chair-caning activities.

About fifteen people were employed in the new facility in its early days. By the late 1930s, more than twenty employees produced kitchen brooms, warehouse brooms, whisk brooms, push brooms, and both hand and deck scrub brushes and mops.

The enterprise established a local theme. Broomcorn used in the manufacturing process came from eastern Washington (and Kansas). Broom and mop handles were made from Washington Douglas fir trees. Other raw materials were sought in the neighborhood.

Always a note of pride, the Lighthouse did not make "cheap" brooms. Superior workmanship and the best materials were standards of the company. Waterfront strikes and downturns in the economy affected sales. Inferior but less expensive brooms were occasionally imported from out of state and manufactured by others. These disappointing episodes were invariably met by renewed marketing efforts, including supportive local newspaper stories. For example, readers were often reminded that the Seattle Lighthouse was a home-grown company, that it was nonprofit, that its leadership came from prominent volunteer women, and that workers did not receive a pension and supported their families from broom-factory earnings.

In the mid-1920s, the Lighthouse became a member of the Seattle Community Chest and Council, later called a Red Feather or United Good Neighbor (UGN) organization. (During the Second World War it took the name Seattle–King County War and Community Chest.) This affiliation allowed the Lighthouse to receive donations collected during annual regional fund drives. Although this was an important source of income, manufacturing operations continued to dominate the balance sheet and turn out a quality product.

After twenty-six years of use the frame structure showed signs of age. A lack of central heating, no automatic sprinkler system (a particular danger, considering the wood shavings and flammable materials being used), and the absence of an employee lounge, lunchroom, or locker room were all troublesome issues. Matters came to a head when the Seattle Fire Department condemned the building in 1949.

Remodeling the old building was a challenge. Besides

incorporating fire-prevention improvements, new rest-rooms and offices, a lounge, a kitchen, and a dining room were also added. Most of the new facilities settled in the second-story addition over the front portion of the building.

Although professional advice was available—thanks to myriad board connections—most renovation funds came from donations by Lighthouse supporters and friends of the board of trustees. Other sources included monies bequeathed to the Lighthouse. The board proudly pointed out that no reconstruction funds were solicited from the public at large or from the Community Chest.

Who was running the Seattle Lighthouse? The volunteer members of the board. Monthly meetings were held and careful minutes were kept. The first board consisted of fifteen members, with the provision that it could be expanded to twenty-five members. Lighthouse work itself was under the supervision of standing committees. In 1950 those committees were known as Building and Grounds, Welfare, Shop, Sales, Entertainment, Community Chest and Council, Publicity, and the Social Center Committee, which directed a new Seattle Social Center for the Blind.

The Social Center for the Blind had clubrooms at 604 University Street, Seattle. Although operating as a separate entity from the Lighthouse, it supported Lighthouse programs with volunteer readers, dance partners (folk and square dancing were favorites), and shoppers. The center's activities included a glee club, a dramatic club, and an orchestra with a piano borrowed from the Home

Undertaking Company. Summer outings and weekly trips were also organized. An auxiliary of the center, called the Venturers, arranged to have members give blood to the King County Blood Bank.

The Social Center hosted the first local marriage between blind partners—Clarence Kales and Dorothy Brunn. A display board at the center, posted in Braille, held travel and shopping tips and general messages. The center had a megascope, which projected large print. A Braille chess set and bingo board were available, and some members practiced on a device to help fry bacon. Speaking of Braille, in 1951, the center held a party to commemorate the 100th anniversary of the death of Louis Braille.

Groups contributing to the Social Center's volunteer contingent were the Seattle Chapter of the National Council of Jewish Women, the Delta Gamma Sorority, the Seattle Junior League, the National Secretaries Association, the Junior Red Cross, and, of course the Lighthouse board.

Additional facilities and funds for blind people in the 1940s and 1950s came from the state of Washington's training center at 104 Twelfth Avenue, Seattle; Lions Clubs; the Washington Protective Association for the Blind; the King County Association for the Blind; and the Occupational Research Club. During the same decades the Seattle Public Library's Division for the Blind became one of only twenty-seven distributing libraries of the Library of Congress. Seattle's Susan J. Henry Library branch at Harvard Avenue and East

Republican Street installed the first room in the nation designed specifically for blind users. It held 7,000 copies of books in Braille and had large reading tables and three listening booths.

In the 1960s, like today, financial help for the Lighthouse came from many sources. For example, besides sharing in a portion of the UGN budget, PONCHO (Patrons of Northwest Civic, Cultural and Charitable Organizations) gave money from their annual auctions to the Lighthouse.

By 1950, new and notable names were on the board roster. The honorary president (and former president) was Mrs. George T. Myers. Mrs. Irving Smith was president; Mrs. Robert E. Lewis, first vice president; Mrs. Leon de Turenne, second vice president (her husband was an outstanding tennis player in the 1920s—Canadian national singles champion, twice Washington state champion, and three times winner of the Seattle title). Other officers: Mrs. Emil G. Sick, third vice president (her husband owned the Rainier Brewery and the Seattle Rainiers baseball club); Mrs. Hugh Purcell, fourth vice president; Mrs. Robert D. Watt, secretary; Mrs. George Parsons, corresponding secretary; and Mrs. Lew V. Day, treasurer. Note that the use of "Mrs." was back in vogue some thirty years after the founders signed the original articles of incorporation with their first names.

A 1950 Seattle Lighthouse report, including a brief history of the organization, received wide distribution. Features of the report included a summary of Lighthouse financial support as follows: ninety percent from product sales; nine percent from the Community Chest and Council; and one percent from membership dues and miscellaneous.

A restatement of Seattle Lighthouse "purposes" was noted in the report: "to maintain a workshop to make the blind self-supporting." That commitment was carried on under the name "Lighthouse Broom Company," employing blind labor except for a supervisory staff of three. Blindness was defined as having "visual acuity of less than 20/200 in their better eye, with corrective glasses."

The Seattle Lighthouse was a union shop for many years. Positions in the broom-making shop were staffed with members of the International Broom & Whisk Makers Union, American Federation of Labor.

Also, the Assortment Sheet Metal Workers Union, Local 383, had an agreement with the Lighthouse. In May 1964, several Handcrest employees who were members of the Sheet Metal Workers Union went on strike, picketing the company's Fourth Avenue South plant. They claimed that "sighted men have been placed on a blind man's job," and that there was an "unequal" distribution of wages and bonuses.

Prior to the 1964 dispute, five blind broom-makers in 1933 had gone on strike because of a reduction in pay. The company responded that an overall deficit (of $1,773) that year had caused a reduction of hours. In the 1960s, union/company discussions centered on the issue of profit sharing.

In the early 1960s, the King County Labor Council threatened to withdraw its support of UGN—a Lighthouse funding source—over the Lighthouse's alleged refusal to sign a union contract. Harry Carr, president of the Labor Council, pointed out that labor helped form the UGN in 1952 and had supported the charitable organization since that time. Pressing the issue, the Labor Council placed the Seattle Lighthouse on its "unfair list." The matter was resolved when the Sheet Metal Workers, Local 383, signed a new contract with the Lighthouse in November 1967. The agreement provided for a fifteen-cent-an-hour wage increase (raising starting pay to $1.85—the top wage was $2.65), several paid holidays, and improved health and welfare benefits.

Using 1950 as a sample measurement of production, the total number of brooms and mops turned out by the labor force was 97,272. Those products were sold throughout western Washington, door to door and through small independent stores. The caning shop rewove seats of cane, fiber rush, rattan slab, flat reed, and hickory. New chair seats totaled 486 in 1950.

In 1960, Lanny Shuman applied to the Lighthouse for the advertised job of truck driver. Shuman had never before been to Seattle. During his job interview with Michael Cariola, Lighthouse executive director, he did not reveal his ignorance of the area. (Cariola's wife participated in the meeting, and from that experience Shuman surmised that Mrs. Cariola had a great deal to say about Lighthouse affairs.) Desperate for work, Shuman promised Lighthouse management that he was "very familiar" with the town. His well-groomed and earnest presence won the day. Each morning he loaded brooms into the truck, drove around the corner to a local service station, and picked up a free city map. Marking his targets in red (hardware stores, small shops, etc.), he then connected the red dots—i.e., his delivery route. Off he went. Every morning he would obtain another free map and similarly mark out his day. Shuman enjoyed working for the Seattle Lighthouse, which was then on Elliott Avenue. He moved on within a year to another opportunity, eventually retiring as a financial analyst with the city of Seattle.

An interesting aspect of Lighthouse work was "welfare services." This category included free instruction in Braille, music, and typing. White canes were distributed at no cost to users. Escort, shopping, and messenger services were offered, and home calls to 200 blind people were accomplished.

Something called "adjustment help" was provided to newly blinded individuals or those with special problems. Examples of "adjustment" consisted of lessons for the blind about how to dress and cook for themselves, how to move about town on their own, and tips on seeking employment. Welfare activities included writing letters and making telephone calls.

Because the 1950 report was written for public as well as in-house use, a list of "don'ts" was presented regarding interacting with the blind. A few examples bear repeating:

* Don't talk to blind people as though they were deaf.
* Don't address a blind person through his or her companion; speak directly to him or her.

* Don't exclaim "marvelous" when he or she does ordinary things.
* Don't leave a door ajar in the vicinity of a blind person.
* Don't push a blind person into a chair; just place his or her hand on the back or arm of the chair.
* Don't treat blind people as abnormal. They are much like you, interested in the same things, able to do most of the same things, and anxious to be accepted as normal members of society.

Space will allow only a sampling of board minutes during the formative years. The following samples of Lighthouse board minutes hint at what was going on forty to seventy years ago:

1929: It was reported that an organization calling itself the Brotherhood for the Determination of the Blind was raising money, assuring prospective buyers that funds would go to the Lighthouse. A motion was made to report this unauthorized activity to the Community Fund (a funding source).

1932: The board heard an explanation for the expenditure of $12 for material and laboratory charges for false teeth (no mention of the recipient), and noted that the dental services of Dr. C.M. Gresham were donated.

1936: Mrs. George T. Myers asked for a list of factory employees' birthdays so each of them could be given a "celebration of some kind" when a birthday occurred.

1956: Mrs. Manson Backus (whose son was blind) reported that she was collecting clippings on new devel-

A workman in the rug-making department operates one of the original rug looms, later replaced by modern equipment purchased with financial support from The Seattle Times.

opments for the blind and would appreciate it if other board members would save similar stories. She also noted that the Social Center for the Blind needed a Braille dictionary.

1961: Mr. Justin Martin reported that $1,500 was received by the Lighthouse from the R.D. Merrill Foundation to be used to purchase equipment.

1962: Mr. Rudolph E. Elmer told of robberies at Seattle Lighthouse. Among the items missing were an intercom system, typewriters, and adding machines. An alarm system was installed shortly thereafter.

1963: Mrs. A. Dean Johnson reported that UGN was asked to stress the social-service aspects of the Lighthouse program in their next campaign rather than repeat their emphasis on broom manufacturing.

1964: Mr. Elmer reported that the Management Committee was seeking to purchase a new building site. Mr. Elmer also noted the interest of both Handcrest and the Lighthouse in several properties. (This was one of several comments in board minutes leading to the 1964 merger of Handcrest and the Seattle Lighthouse, which is discussed in Chapter 6.)

Lighthouse Trustees organized events to find support and draw attention to their mission. One such celebration was the annual Christmas party for the blind. In the 1940s, those parties were often held in Cathedral Hall of St. Mark's Cathedral. Mary Louise Rochester Roderick, an accomplished pianist and singer (and the aunt of this book's author), often provided entertainment at the Christmas affairs, trading keyboard duties with board member "Kit" (Mrs. Emil) Sick.

In 1946, at the Bon Marche department store, trustees hosted showings of objects made at Seattle Lighthouse, including checkerboards, Chinese checkers, and other board games; thermometers; and the usual array of cane products, brooms, and mops.

The old Benjamin Franklin Hotel (now absorbed by Westin Hotels) was the site of a "sumptuous" August 17, 1959, cocktail party organized by the trustees that preceded the opening-night performance of *My Fair Lady*.

(The Alan Jay Lerner and Frederick Loewe musical was on the road for the first time since its New York opening in 1956.) Dinner at the hotel's famous Outrigger restaurant was included. Principal hosts for the event were Mesdames Richard A. Olson, Clarence M. Ambrose, Robert Isaacson, William K. Blethen, and Paul Friedlander. Both *The Seattle Times* and the *Seattle Post-Intelligencer* gave full-page coverage to the event, including noting that the party "Will be Loverly" (the *P-I*). The event was something of a coup, and was an example of the board's clout.

Lighthouse trustees produced a similar event on June 14, 1961. It coincided with the opening of *Fiorello!* at the Orpheum Theatre and included a lavish Italian dinner in the Olympic Hotel's Grand Ballroom. Co-chairs for the event were Mrs. J. Collins Lloyd and Mrs. William K. Blethen, with Mrs. Robert Denny Watt, president of the board.

Board meetings were held within the comfortable surroundings of women's social clubs, especially the exclusive Sunset Club, a 1915 Georgian treasure designed by architect Joseph S. Cote (who also designed St. James Cathedral, Seattle's Roman Catholic cathedral). Meetings were occasionally held at Lighthouse premises and in private homes. Whatever the venue, trustees were thorough and timely in monitoring and supporting Lighthouse programs.

During preparation of this book, the author heard from children of former board members. Memories of their mothers' involvement at the Seattle Lighthouse

● MRS. ROBERT DENNY WATT (left) and Mrs. Lawrence McLellan fill cups from coffee urn at Lighthouse for the Blind. Remodeling the kitchen at the Lighthouse was one of main projects discussed at annual meeting held Tuesday at Sunset Club. Mrs. Watt was elected secretary and Mrs. McLellan is second vice president. Organization is United Good Neighbor agency.

A newspaper article from the Seattle
Post-Intelligencer, February 11, 1953

remain clear. In many cases, the example set by their mothers helped establish their own lifelong patterns in charitable work.

Mary Stalter Radsch called from New York to describe how her mother, former board president Mary Grace Stalter, was well organized in everything she undertook.

Robert M. Arnold retains clear memories of his mother, Grace Heffernan Arnold, attending board meetings and discussing Lighthouse matters at home. (Her husband, Lawrence Arnold, was chairman of Seattle-First National Bank.) Grace Arnold also raised money to send blind persons for training with guide dogs. Robert Arnold's former wife and mother-in-law, both named Mary McClellan, were also on the board.

The Manson Backus family, long active in Seattle's business and cultural affairs, is proud of Mrs. Backus's contribution as a Lighthouse board member. The family of Helen Berkman Blumenthal was especially interested in the Seattle Lighthouse, because Blumenthal devoted her adult life to programs for the blind.

Helen Blumenthal's story is unique. She was president of the Sisterhood of Temple de Hirsch (in Seattle) in the early 1930s and was on the Sisterhood National Board. During this time she met Rabbi Michael Aaronsohn, a blind field representative of the Union of American Hebrew Congregations. He encouraged Blumenthal to study Braille, which later emerged as a program to translate books and articles for blind students at the University of Washington. Performing their Braille translations by hand—"one punch at a time"— Blumenthal's committee made many books available to the blind. Blumenthal bought the first Braille typewriter in the Seattle area and helped form the Library for the Blind, later part of the King County Library system. That facility is now called the Washington Talking Book and Braille Library and is administered by the Seattle Public Library.

*A Seattle Lighthouse building occupying the present site of
Seattle Post-Intelligencer offices, 1920s-1950s. Photo
courtesy of the Pemco Webster & Stevens Collection at the
Museum of History & Industry*

On September 13, 1929, novelist and playwright Edna
Ferber (her novels include *Giant* and *Showboat*, which
were made into films, and she co-wrote *Dinner at Eight*, a
great Broadway success, with George S. Kaufman),
answering a letter from Blumenthal, wrote that her
(Ferber's) father was blind. She also expressed apprecia-
tion to Blumenthal for translating Ferber's book of short
stories, *Mother Knows Best* (1927), into Braille.

Upon Helen Blumenthal's 1969 retirement from forty
years on the Lighthouse board, Mrs. Kermit Rosen, Sr.,
her daughter, became a trustee. Helen was elected to
honorary board membership and continued her work for
the Social Center for the Blind in Seattle.

Despite notable successes and generous publicity, by the
late 1950s it was clear to the board that the Lighthouse

was struggling to succeed in its efforts to generate sufficient revenues from the manufacture of crafts, principally the durable brooms. Without dissent, discussions commenced regarding a merger with Handcrest, Inc., a non-profit organization employing blind people and others with disabilities.

A new and exciting path lay ahead for The Lighthouse for the Blind.

CHAPTER 4
National Focus

The Seattle Lighthouse, although independent in inception, activities, and growth, has for many decades been associated with national and international trends and ideas supporting people who are blind, Deaf-Blind, and have other disabilities. The Lighthouse's status as a pioneering Pacific Northwest institution is established. Less understood is its cooperative role in wider organizations.

Historical perspective indicates that employment for blind people began in the early nineteenth century. Prior to that they—and others with disabilities—were generally recipients of charity, pity, and abuse. As the Industrial Revolution grew in England, on the Continent, and then in the United States, the "sheltered" workshop was introduced as a step to help blind individuals find gainful employment. Special schools for blind children were founded, followed by training schools.

Early records show that the Perkins Institute for the Blind in Boston was the first "sheltered" training and educational facility in the United States. However, it may have been a London, England, cellar where the first independent workshop for the blind was established. In the 1890s, Overbrook School for the Blind in Philadelphia and the Pennsylvania Working Home for the Blind combined to house and employ blind persons. Similar regional institutions arose across the country.

Peter J. Salmon, a graduate of the Perkins Institute, grasped the possibilities of these changes. His knowledge and devotion to the blind were well known in the early 1900s. Directing his attention to the U.S. Congress, Salmon testified on behalf of workshops for the blind. The product he had in mind, and one that caught the attention of virtually every workshop for the blind in the nation, was brooms. In fact, the National Broom Manufacturers Association endorsed his proposals, with the national government cited as the principal buyer of that famous product.

At this point, the American Foundation for the Blind, under the leadership of M.C. Migel, president, and Dr. Robert B. Irwin, executive director, became active in lobbying Congress. The combination of these forceful, informed individuals resulted in the 1938 introduction of a bill (S.2819) by U.S. Representative James J. Lanzetta, D-New York, to "create a commission on purchases of blind-made products . . . " The next step was to find federal markets for blind-made products—again, brooms— which resulted in a visit by Messrs. Migel, Irwin, and Salmon to the Bureau of Prisons, Department of Justice.

During the flurry of bills introduced in early New Deal days—the mid-1930s—a number of "experimental" ideas were thrown into the hopper. Among those innovations, U.S. Senator Robert F. Wagner, Sr., D-New York, and U.S. Representative Caroline O'Day, D-New York, with the urging of Mr. Migel and others, introduced legislation related to "workshops." Using brooms and mops as legislative levers, so to speak, the proposed bill required: (1) purchases by the Federal Government; (2) a provision that brooms be supplied at a fair market price; and (3) establishment of a committee to determine the fair market price of brooms.

It was not coincidental that New Yorkers dominated the political spectrum in the 1930s and 1940s, with direct results for disabled Americans. President Franklin D. Roosevelt was a former New York governor. He sought the bulk of his advisers from his home turf. For example, U.S. Senator Robert F. Wagner, Sr., a Roosevelt confidant, was author of the Social Security Act of 1935. Wagner served in Congress from 1929 to 1949. U.S. Representative Caroline Love Goodwin O'Day, a staunch supporter of the New Deal, was a member of Congress from 1935 to 1943. Wagner and O'Day sponsored the Wagner-O'Day Act (WOD), of direct benefit to blind persons.

The Great Depression resulted in not only the overwhelming election of Franklin D. Roosevelt, but also a growing public sensitivity toward social obligations and problems. After more testimony, and the addition of minor amendments, "An Act to Create a Committee on Purchases of Blind-Made Products and for other Purposes" was introduced, passing the Senate on March 31st and the House on June 13th, 1938.

To qualify for government orders, the workshops had to be certified as actual employers of blind labor. High standards of quality and adherence to government specifications were added as components to the act.

The Wagner-O'Day Act became the law of the land after being signed by President Roosevelt on June 25th, 1938. The Committee on Purchases of Blind-Made Products was empowered to determine the fair market price. It comprised representatives from the following agencies: the Paymaster General of the Navy, the Quartermaster General of the Army, the Treasury Department, the Department of the Interior, the Department of Commerce, and private citizens. Private presidential appointments, besides several trusted friends of FDR, included pioneer lobbyist M.C. Migel of the American Foundation for the Blind.

With the door open for the first time to federally approved employment opportunities for blind workers,

Joan Ladeburg completes a sponge mop for sale to federal customers under the Javits-Wagner-O'Day Act.

other products they could manufacture came to mind: cocoa mats, deck swabs, pillowcases, mattresses, rubber mats, rugs, ironing-board covers, tea towels, leather belts, billfolds, and suspenders. In later years, as was amply demonstrated by Lighthouse products made for both private industry and the Defense Department, the sky was the limit.

U.S. Senator Jacob K. Javits, sponsor of later amendments to the Wagner-O'Day Act, rose through New York Mayor Fiorello La Guardia's reform movement, despite being a Republican. In 1946, Javits became the first New York Republican since 1923 to be elected to the U.S. House of Representatives. A dramatic expansion of the WOD occurred in 1971, when Javits, now a U.S. senator, introduced amendments to include other disabled workers besides blind persons. The Seattle Lighthouse played an indirect role in this change when Washington state's Democratic U.S. Senator Warren G. Magnuson (in addition to Senator Jennings Randolph, D-West Virginia) added his sponsorship to Javits's amendments, expanding it from eighty-three to 600 additional workshops. This quantum jump reached approximately 40,000 employees, many of them severely disabled—an explosion in help for citizens who had historically been virtually ignored by government. The expanded program was (and is) known as the Javits-Wagner-O'Day Act (JWOD).

As a result of the new Javits amendments, the Committee on Purchases of Blind-made Products expanded its name to the Committee for Purchase from People who are Blind or Severely Disabled. All U.S. citizens with disabilities who worked at NIB (National Industries for the Blind) or NISH (formerly National Industries for the Severely Handicapped) agencies now came under the same umbrella.

Among the most frequently asked questions about JWOD are the following:

Q: *What are the advantages of contracting under JWOD (for federal customers only)?*

A: Besides having the satisfaction of helping individuals and families with disabilities, high-quality products and services are offered at reasonable and competitive prices;

Q: *Where can a list of JWOD products be found?*

A: On the JWOD Web site (www.jwod.gov) and by contacting the Seattle Lighthouse directly or one of its base supply centers (discussed later in this chapter).

Q: *Can nonprofit agencies bid competitively on federal contracts?*

A: Yes, under the same conditions as other commercial offers.

Q: *When are JWOD prices for products and services changed?*

A: Usually annually.

Q: *Do JWOD products and services meet current environmental and recycling standards?*

A: Yes. All such products and services must meet federal mandates, including those with environmental impact.

Congress continues to monitor and modify JWOD. Wage issues constantly arise, as do matters pertaining to promoting disabled workers to higher positions. The latter issue was addressed in part by the annual Peter J. Salmon "Blind Worker of the Year" Award, given by NIB to "a direct labor manufacturing or service contract employee who is legally blind."

The Seattle Lighthouse boasts the highest number of national Peter J. Salmon Award winners among all similar organizations. Jerry McIsaac was chosen in 1970. In 1974, Arne Paul Nermo, a machinist, won this prestigious honor in a nationwide competition over nominees from eighty-five other workshops. Lillian Meske, the first Deaf-Blind winner, took the award in 1978. In 2000, Lighthouse machinist Roosevelt Stevenson won the award (Stevenson came to the Lighthouse in 1996 and still finds time to mentor neighborhood children, work for his church, and give talks to Boys & Girls Clubs). The Lighthouse continues to nominate employees for the Peter J. Salmon Award.

A different but equally prestigious honor, the Milton J. Samuelson Career Achievement Award (Milton J. Samuelson, a former NIB executive director, was known for his efforts to create meaningful employment opportunities for people with visual impairments), was given to Seattle Lighthouse employee Jenné Arnold in 2002. The award is "designed to recognize the accomplishments of people who are blind and employed in a NIB-associated agency above the direct labor level and below the top administrative level." Arnold is Deaf-Blind as a result of

Usher syndrome. She was selected for her leadership in the blindness field while working in an indirect labor position.

In a sideways step from the federal government to military families, NIB initiated steps in 1948 to broaden the market for commercially interesting blind-made products through sales in military commissaries.

By the mid-1950s, blindness agencies, including The Seattle Lighthouse for the Blind, had proved that they could meet rigid government product specifications and maintain high quality. As a result of this capability, and recent changes in the distribution of blind-made JWOD products, the Lighthouse today operates four base supply centers on military bases: McChord Air Force Base, in Tacoma, Washington; Fort Lewis, also in Tacoma; Naval Air Station Fallon in Nevada (this is the training center for the famous Blue Angels and employs about 2,000 support personnel); and the Space and Naval Warfare Systems Center in San Diego.

The Lighthouse also operates McChord's Hazardous Materials Pharmacy. Karen Kidd, Seattle Lighthouse director of logistics and base supply centers, notes that McChord has an excellent environmental record and keeps a close eye on hazardous materials. The Lighthouse is constantly investigating product sales opportunities on other military reservations throughout the United States.

In the late 1970s, with the cooperation of NIB, groups of blind workers were placed in local plants for training opportunities alongside sighted workers. Similar cooperative efforts followed, with considerable success. The NIB board of directors made a 1985 declaration affirming that "competitive placement" of workshop employees is the highest form of upward mobility.

The Seattle Lighthouse staff is aware that better management is necessary to facilitate upward mobility and to compete with sighted industry. The continuing rise in sales under the JWOD program has been a favorable omen, but improved management skills and collaborative and cooperative workplace conditions have also contributed to sales.

The term "sheltered" workshops is occasionally a subject of discussion. The Seattle Lighthouse has left that early craft-making designation far behind. The shift has been made from crafts such as brooms and baskets to molded plastic products, metal stampings, and aircraft parts. Also, the increasing use of computers equipped with Braille and speech outputs, and computer numerically controlled manufacturing equipment, is under scrutiny by NIB, NISH, JWOD, and Lighthouse management and employees.

The Lighthouse for the Blind is aware that what worked yesterday may be irrelevant tomorrow. Knowing more about regional and world markets, economics, technological changes on the horizon, evolving attitudes toward management and human resource issues, and new physical and psychological treatments for disabilities, motivates and challenges Lighthouse leadership and employees.

CHAPTER 5
Wings of Boeing

When Yale engineer William Edward Boeing met Navy
Lieutenant Commander Conrad Westervelt at the
Seattle's Men's University Club in the early 1900s, it
resulted in a friendship, a business relationship, and a
frightening but exhilarating flight with a barnstorming
pilot on the Fourth of July, 1915. Their fledgling company, after six months of existence, had less than $4,000 in
the bank, unpaid bills totaling $7,500, and assets valued
at $46,000. None of these facts hinted at the company's
future success or its later inclination to consider corpo-
rate philanthropy.

Although The Boeing Company was too late to contribute airplanes to the Great War, the 1920s brought
new challenges: flying boats and airmail service. These
learning experiences—and a first-rate engineering
cadre—caused the company to find itself in a unique
position to build United States aircraft for World War II.

Virtually all of Boeing's early growth occurred at
Boeing Field, Seattle's southern boundary (and at one
time a bicycle velodrome and motor-car race field).
About the same time, and soon after the 1918 incorporation of The Lighthouse for the Blind, Boeing and the

Lighthouse were finding their respective—but obviously dissimilar—paths in Seattle's business and cultural communities. While Boeing's expansion exploded, primarily during the war years, the Seattle Lighthouse moved forward deliberately under the able direction of an all-female board of trustees, several of whom were married to Boeing executives.

After the war, Boeing's energetic entry into the booming field of civil aviation, and the company's continuing defense contracts, allowed the growing firm to think seriously about participating in charitable, cultural, and civic activities. The Boeing name began to appear on the rolls of Seattle's major cultural organizations.

Rudolph E. "Rudy" Elmer joined Handcrest, Inc., in 1951 as a salesman. It soon became clear to Rudy that Handcrest, a nonprofit organization driven by handmade products, needed to find new opportunities, perhaps based on new technology. Elmer, a former public school teacher and principal, opened the Yellow Pages to find local companies that might contract with Handcrest. One of his first "cold calls" was to PACCAR, the giant truck manufacturer in Bellevue, Washington.

By 1970, Lighthouse workers were producing hose assemblies, cutting insulation, and making U bolts for securing braking-system air tanks to the trucks. Lighthouse work for PACCAR soared to 1,250,000 hose assemblies in 1977. Completed assemblies were tested to withstand pressures up to 1,500 pounds per square inch. A PACCAR newsmagazine story about its relationship with Seattle Lighthouse noted that "at least 75 percent of the employees are legally blind." The story pointed out that the Seattle Lighthouse also employed "mentally retarded" blind workers and several who were deaf and blind. It continued by mentioning "quality products" and "employees [who] are experiencing the satisfaction that comes from a job well done and an independent income."

Even before Elmer contacted PACCAR, he had formed a connection between Boeing and Handcrest. Boeing documents refer to the year 1951, when the company "became involved in providing a few simple jobs to an agency working with blind people." That agency was, of course, Handcrest (which in 1964 merged with the Seattle Lighthouse; see Chapter 6). Elmer was at first discouraged because of Boeing's complicated manufacturing processes. This did not stop his frequent

visits to Seattle's Boeing plant to develop a working agreement. In fact, his trips became so commonplace that Boeing issued him a permanent visitor's pass.

Elmer later described his burgeoning relation-

Rudolph Elmer,
executive director
from 1950 through
1979 (1960s)

ship with the airplane giant: "In order for us to manufacture aircraft parts, using Boeing's or our machinery, we needed Boeing to supply us with the tooling for each part." Soon, there were daily deliveries of finished products to Boeing, and return deliveries with new loads of raw materials. Elmer emphasized that the Boeing relationship was successful because quality Handcrest products were made according to strict specifications. Among the first Handcrest Boeing products were small aluminum clips used in the KC-97 Stratocruiser.

Elmer enjoyed recalling that under Boeing president William Allen everyone "punched in," including the chief. All Boeing employees flew coach in those days, he remembers. He was also surprised more than once when Allen visited Handcrest unannounced.

In the early 1960s, the Handcrest building at Twelfth Avenue and Yesler Way, despite utilization of its basement rooms, was not large enough to accommodate Boeing's growing orders. At this point larger space was found on Fourth Avenue near Spokane Street, in Seattle.

Handcrest's Fourth Avenue South location (1960s)

Encouraged by Elmer, Boeing began to send representatives to the Lighthouse on a regular basis. Seeing
disabled employees turn out Boeing parts efficiently and
in a well-run workplace convinced the large company
that they had a solid contract. To this day, a reserved
parking spot near the Lighthouse's Plum Street main
entrance has a sign that says, "BOEING."

In 1968, Boeing evaluated its Philanthropic Program.
Noting that its longest relationship was with Handcrest,
and that it had contracts with five other workshops, it
spelled out features of the program. The Boeing Philanthropic Committee met once a month, with a representative of its Materiel Department as chairman. Committee
members included representatives from Tool and Production Planning, Industrial Engineering, and Production Control. At these meetings, jobs for each of the
workshops were selected, matching job requirements with
the known capabilities of each shop.

Maintaining a level workload, the Boeing paper states,
is of singular importance to both Boeing and the shops.
Because the aircraft industry is constantly changing, the
company must frequently search for new jobs to sustain
reasonable loads. It also referred to occasional schedule
and quality problems, and noted that despite "very capable" shop management, disabled workers need consistent
help and technical support.

Boeing concluded, in its March 28, 1968, assessment
(written by Eldon Coberly), that the Philanthropic Program "has been mutually advantageous to the Boeing
Company and our philanthropic suppliers. It provides

work to those who are rated industrially unemployable, and who would otherwise have to depend on welfare or charity. We are receiving quality parts on schedule at a competitive price while providing a worthwhile service to the community."

Although Boeing philanthropy was introduced and encouraged by Bill Allen, the actual monitoring of the program fell to Stan Little. Little had joined Boeing in 1944 as an engineer but gravitated toward administrative detail and labor negotiations. He was fair, patient, and had a sense of humor.

Little added his own comments to Coberly's summary at the October 7, 1968, annual meeting of the General Council of Workshops for the Blind, in Seattle. Noting that Rudy Elmer had asked him to make a few remarks about Boeing's Philanthropic Program, Little opened with the comment that "good intentions alone do not make a philanthropic program successful, but they are at least the starting point." His talk pointed out that the company had learned from its relationship with Handcrest and other "workshops," and that the program had proven to be a "worthwhile endeavor."

Little noted several major elements of the program, including pricing in line with Boeing estimates, and adherence to quality standards and schedules. The shops, he pointed out, had low overhead costs and managers who could organize jobs and operations for minimum cost and maximum efficiency.

Summing up, Little reminded his audience that "once a company commits itself to support a philanthropic endeavor, many factors come into play. People up and down the organization line have an inherent interest in getting the most and best for the company dollars they spend."

Also in 1968, Boeing was honored by the National Industries for the Blind (NIB) for its philanthropic program of subcontracting to workshops employing disabled persons. Although Handcrest/Seattle Lighthouse pioneered that relationship, and was the largest of the subject agencies, there were others, including the United Cerebral Palsy Center, Orion Industries, Pioneer Industries, Firlands, and Skills Industries.

That same year, George "Jake" Jacobson left Boeing to join the Seattle Lighthouse as sales manager. In 1979 he became executive director. The Rudy Elmer period of innovation and growth continued under Jacobson's leadership. Jacobson introduced new ideas to meet technological changes of the 1980s. During 1982–1983, as president of the General Council of Workshops for the Blind, Jacobson was frequently on the road, very much missing his hometown of Seattle, but nevertheless learning a great deal about how other blindness agencies operated.

In 1990, under Jacobson's direction, and partly as a result of the Boeing relationship, the Lighthouse saw the rise of a bustling manufacturing center in Rainier Valley and the introduction of technology on a large scale. Strategies also included a full-time effort to reach both government and consumer groups. Projected sales for 1990 were $15 million, up from $11.4 million in 1989. Of

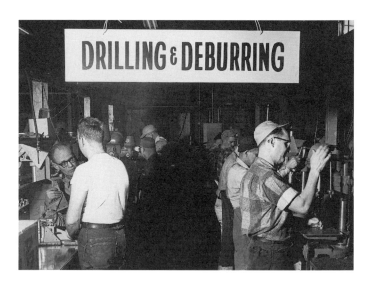

*Handcrest's Twelfth Avenue and Yesler Way location.
Arne Nermo (left) and Frank Copeland (right) make parts
for The Boeing Company.*

378 Lighthouse employees, 75 percent were visually impaired. Jake pointed out that the Seattle Lighthouse ranked third in the nation in sales by nonprofit agencies employing people who are blind, and was the largest such agency in the West.

The Boeing component remained strong, as the Lighthouse continued to produce metal airplane parts. Jacobson identified "8,000 jobs we can do for Boeing and we have a backlog of 1,000 [jobs] at any given time." The Boeing contract provided work for 100 blind people in 1990, mostly manufacturing aluminum parts, plus some rubber or foam seals. Seattle Lighthouse produced 1.75 million parts for Boeing in 1989.

Following the New York City terrorist attacks of September 11, 2001, Bruce Walker, then board chairman of the Seattle Lighthouse, wrote in his 2003 annual report that many things had changed in the aircraft industry. A sharp reduction of Lighthouse labor hours occurred, compelling Lighthouse management to make reductions in staff and affecting approximately thirty blind and Deaf-Blind workers. Additionally, reduced revenue necessitated cuts in training and support service programs.

Walker added that the Boeing Company "has been a wonderful partner, supporting our program for more than 50 years." The sudden changes, however, served as a wake-up call. It was clear that the Lighthouse would have to double its efforts to explore new products and services it could provide. Walker suggested that strategies for the new millennium should include "the continued development of community support, growth of revenue and employment opportunities through customer-focused initiatives, more effective sales and marketing of products, new product development, expansion of Base Service Center activities and locations, and commercial partnerships."

Raymond W. Haman, an attorney who joined the Lighthouse board in 1962 and later served as board chair, and who has a near-photographic memory of Seattle Lighthouse history, pointed out in 2003 that Boeing's contribution is virtually incalculable. In the past, Ray pointed out that Boeing funded 80 percent of Lighthouse rehabilitation services, separate from its manufacturing contracts. This core activity has been of enormous benefit to Lighthouse employees.

Don Helsel, Seattle Lighthouse director of manufacturing, came directly to the point: Boeing's support was introduced at a critical time. The company's evolving technology and training helped the Seattle Lighthouse diversify and prepare for the future. Helsel estimated that generally 60 percent of Lighthouse work and activity during the 1970s and 1980s resulted from Boeing contracts.

During a tour of the Lighthouse's Boeing assembly area one sees an array of products reflecting the ever-changing needs of the big company. Sun visors, moisture barriers, curtain hangers, junction boxes, and items from the machine shop reflect current (2004) Boeing needs.

Bob Johnson, Seattle Lighthouse vice president for sales and marketing, put the Boeing-Lighthouse connection in another perspective. He pointed out that, as a result of Boeing contracts, quality assurance and training became core Lighthouse competencies. He also stated that the Boeing relationship moved the Lighthouse from a craft-based operation to a manufacturing operation, charting a new course for The Seattle Lighthouse for the Blind.

The Boeing Company and the Seattle Lighthouse share a strong, long-standing partnership. While the vagaries of international events, economics, and new technology will bring changes and challenges to the relationship, the vision and the commitment are firm. Both organizations, part of the fabric of Seattle for more than eighty years, will continue working together to create opportunities for blind people to live independent and self-sufficient lives and to receive the benefits of steady, high-quality employment, upward mobility, world-class training, and cutting-edge technology. Those goals are intact and will be strengthened.

CHAPTER 6
Mergers & Beyond

Handcrest, Inc., of Seattle, Washington, described itself to the general public in a 1950s house brochure as a "non-profit, private enterprise [that] markets products of the sightless and handicapped who have learned their skills at the Washington State Rehabilitation and Training Center for the Blind." (The center was then at the northeast corner of Twelfth Avenue and Yesler Way, Seattle).

Handcrest had reason to be proud of its efforts to make blind employees self-supporting. The ten-page brochure was an early effort to draw attention to a largely ignored and misunderstood part of the population—while simultaneously marketing its products.

As noted in previous chapters, Handcrest merged with the Seattle Lighthouse in 1964. The result was a tighter business operation that successfully evolved and changed over the years. Following is the story of how that merger came about and how it reshaped and redirected the activities and products of the venerable Lighthouse for the Blind.

The story begins with the establishment of a fledgling training center in 1937 by the Vancouver School for the Blind. Two years later, in 1939, a group of Seattle busi-

Handcrest products (1950s through 1960s) Handcrest's hand-woven textiles were sold through department stores nationwide.

ness executives formed a separate nonprofit organization to act as a sales outlet for products from the training center. Serving without pay, this group consisted of Neal E. Tourtellotte, head of a building specialties company and later director of the Northwest Regional Office of the Small Business Administration, and Dr. Purman Dorman, a well-known Seattle eye, ear, nose, and throat specialist. Dorman was an original member of the Eye Bank of Sight Restoration in the state and on the advisory board of the National Society for the Prevention of Blindness.

Neal Tourtellotte asked his brother-in-law, attorney George V. Powell, to draw up papers for the new organization. Powell remained involved with Handcrest legal matters during its growth period, and members of his law firm (today known as Lane Powell Spears Lubersky) are still active in Lighthouse affairs. Tourtellotte and Dorman helped manage the company into the 1950s.

Other founders included Philip Weyerhaeuser, Jr., president of the Weyerhaeuser Timber Company; Harry Hartman, a blind bookseller; William S. Street, president of Frederick & Nelson; Francis Pearson, also blind, who was chairman of the Public Service Commission of the State of Washington; and Hector Escobosa, president of I. Magnin & Co. (In his 135-page 1948 book, *Seattle Story*, Escobosa wrote that he hopes his book "will help to remind Seattleites, and show the world outside, that those of us who live here have much for which we can be thankful.")

Also signing Handcrest's 1939 Articles of Incorporation were Theo Mays and Mrs. Dwight Mead, at that time the only woman board member.

Later directors included Raymond W. Haman, an attorney with Evans, McLaren, Lane, Powell & Beeks. Haman, a former board chairman, remains a Lighthouse trustee in 2004 and a helpful link to the history of both Handcrest and the Seattle Lighthouse.

Other directors were John F. Lubetich, financial secretary of the Sheet Metal Workers Union, Local 383; Michael W. Galante, owner of Seattle Knitting Mills, Inc.; Fuller R. Hale, executive director of the Social Center for the Blind; Jack Utz and Thomas Lukanovic of Frederick & Nelson; and Richard A. Maginot, of The Bon Marche. Other distinguished members were Ferdinand Schmitz, president of Berger Engineering Company; Merrill W. Scott of Allied Stores Corporation; and William W. Berry of The Boeing Company, and a current Lighthouse Board member.

Handcrest products were sold through retail stores, by direct mail and telephone, by door-to-door salespeople (all men in those days), and by contract. At first the com-

A Handcrest employee operates a press brake for Boeing parts (1950s).

pany specialized in metal fabrication and hand-woven products. Customers for the Metal Products Division—air compressors, lathes, wire strippers, punch presses, and more—included Boeing and other Seattle-area firms. On the other hand, the Hand-Woven Products Division—men's neckties, skirt lengths, stoles, draperies, place mats, rugs, etc.—found customers from Illinois to Alaska to Detroit to Los Angeles.

Rudolph Elmer, managing director of Handcrest, filled his car with samples and called on customers from Washington to California. Senior Lighthouse employees remember hearing stories about Elmer and his wife, May, selling ties out of the back of their old Mercury car. According to Elmer's own journal, his road stops during the 1940s and 1950s included Malcolm Brock Co., in Bakersfield; Betty Pritchard Baby Shop, in Fullerton; and May Company, in Los Angeles, all in California. In Oregon he visited Mann's Department Store, in Medford; Mathan's, in Pendleton; and Young Set, in The Dalles. In

Washington state, Elmer's customers included Bremer's Department Store, in Bremerton (Bremerton is named for this family); Columbia River Mercantile Company, in Longview; and Schoenfeld's, in Tacoma.

Hella Skowronski was appointed designer for soft-lines at Handcrest in 1962. She created patterns that blind employees followed while hand-weaving Handcrest products. Skowronski was a member of the Fashion Group, and her designs were featured at Century 21, the 1962 Seattle World's Fair.

Handcrest's main office was at one time 1514 Tenth Avenue, Seattle. Later a "workshop" and hand-weaving operation was at 104 Twelfth Avenue, just off Yesler Way. Several "home weavers" were supervised from this location.

Martha Haugen of Anacortes, Washington, recounted her memories as a twelve-year-old girl when she accompanied her blind grandmother to the Yesler weaving operation. Her grandmother, Elisa Azna Grammer, made place mats for Handcrest during the 1940s. Young Martha looked forward to having lunch with her grandmother and was fascinated with her hand skills, employed in the manufacturing process. Haugen owns and cherishes several of her grandmother's place mats.

Handcrest and the state's Rehabilitation and Training Center for the Blind (RTCB) were very different entities but had a similar goal: providing employment opportunities for blind people. Handcrest, a nonprofit business organization, was formed to market products produced by blind people. Those workers, in turn, were trained by the RTCB. As Ray Haman pointed out, "Marketing is only possible if people are willing to buy what is being produced." A case in point was wicker baskets, an early product of RTCB-trained people, which were not selling. Instead, they were filling up a local warehouse.

Coordinating manufacturing and selling became an obvious function to both Handcrest and the RTCB. This led to the two organizations jointly occupying a building at Twelfth Avenue and Yesler Way in the early 1950s. The upper level housed looms and the sewing operation. The machine shop and general offices were on the lower level.

In the mid-1950s, RTCB employees came under the Handcrest umbrella, thereby becoming eligible for disability and retirement benefits. Blind employees were pleased with their private-sector payroll checks, and Handcrest board and management became accustomed to supervising blind workers.

Lighthouse machine shop at current location (1970s)

On April 1, 1953, Handcrest, Inc., signed an agreement with the state of Washington and thereafter assumed the role of a quasi-state agency under the aegis of the Department of Public Assistance.

The Handcrest board developed company "Objects and Purposes" in May 1957: "To aid in the rehabilitation of physically handicapped persons who have received adequate training in handcrafts and who are engaged in the production of saleable merchandise under proper supervision by doing all things generally necessary, proper, or convenient to assist such handicapped persons." This was followed by a list of specific tasks, including receiving merchandise, promoting sales, investigating new products, undertaking design and manufacturing of saleable items, conducting advertising, and directing a sales force.

Albert D. Rosellini was governor of the state of Washington during the later Handcrest years, including the Handcrest/Lighthouse merger days. His appointed director of the State Department of Public Assistance, George C. Starlund, played a key role in the Handcrest/Lighthouse affair.

In an early 2004 conversation, Rosellini described why he and Starlund took a special interest in Handcrest. Just prior to announcing his first race for governor, in 1956, Rosellini had learned, largely through his work as a state senator, that Washington state's hospitals, prisons and similar institutions were in bad shape, and many had lost or were about to lose their accreditation. During his two terms as governor (1957 to 1965) he spent a great deal of time and money improving state institutions, which resulted in accreditation for all of them, and several achieved positive national recognition. He affirmed that those efforts included concern for state facilities serving disabled citizens. Rudy Elmer, former manager of both Handcrest and the Lighthouse, remembered Governor Rosellini's personal participation in several discussions about Handcrest.

Several years after Handcrest and the RTCB merged, it became clear to the Handcrest board and to Elmer that the new operation could be self-supporting. Some state employees had reservations about "losing" the blind operation, and the state attorney general's office raised the issue of the state constitution's prohibition against "gifts of state property." It was mutually agreed that Handcrest and the RTCB would be parties to a "friendly" lawsuit to resolve these issues.

The 1962 "friendly" suit focused on disposition of Handcrest's operating reserve account. Once he learned that Handcrest would be self-supporting, public assistance director George Starlund, with the backing of Governor Rosellini, pressed for the independence of Handcrest.

Ray Haman, who was present during most of these meetings, recalled that Starlund had recently learned of an imminent federal grant to build and operate a Seattle-based facility serving blind people from several Pacific Northwest states. The projected facility would provide basic living skills and related training to the newly blind. This new development would essentially leave vocational training and employment to groups like Handcrest. In other words, the tides were favorable to separate Handcrest from the state.

In its decision the court wrote that the department would likely not prevail in the suit, and that both parties were "desirous of settling and compromising the . . . action in order to facilitate the taking over by Handcrest of the operation of the workshop and handweaving operation independently of the Department."

On May 1, 1962, Superior Court Judge Charles T. Wright, in dismissing the suits, noted that both parties agreed to a settlement. The department delivered a quit claim bill of sale conveying to Handcrest the department's "right, title and interest" in Handcrest's operating reserve account.

Following the settlement Handcrest purchased the state-owned manufacturing equipment and furnishings for their appraised value and moved its operation to 3314 Fourth Avenue South, Seattle. The divorce was not a clean break: the Department continued to work closely with Handcrest, referring clients for vocational training and employment.

The decks were now clear, so to speak, for the 1964 merger of Handcrest and the Seattle Lighthouse. Talks had been under way for more than a year, led by Rudy Elmer, executive director of Handcrest, who was a "loaned executive" to the Lighthouse. Rudy had also brought along his assistant, Hanako "Hank" Nakagawa.

On November 25, 1964, Ferdinand Schmitz, president of Handcrest, Inc., and Justin Martin, president of the Seattle Lighthouse, announced the merger agreement. The merger's purpose was described as follows: " . . . to provide increased employment for the blind through an expansion of 'on the job training' and in upgrading of rehabilitation services."

A press release at the time noted that the name "Lighthouse for the Blind, Inc." would be retained for the new organization. A twenty-seven-person volunteer board would be selected from both groups. Handcrest would continue its light sheet-metal work at Fourth Avenue South, while the hand-woven products would be located at 131 Elliott Avenue West, Seattle (Lighthouse premises).

The Seattle Lighthouse changed dramatically following the merger. The new volunteer board now included a number of experienced Seattle businesspeople. Several women members of the previous Lighthouse board remained, but the thrust was tilted toward manufacturing, rather than crafts. Accepted business practices were established, including accounting, human resources, shop safety, and general management procedures.

In 1966, Lighthouse board members Ferdinand Schmitz, Mrs. Paul Friedlander, and Mrs. Max Wyman broke ground at Twenty-fifth Avenue South and South Plum Street, Seattle, for a 40,000-square-foot building. The new Lighthouse headquarters and manufacturing facility were budgeted at $404,000.

Lighthouse facilities were to be co-located with a next-door city-sponsored complex for the housing, treatment, employment, and rehabilitation of disabled persons. The combined Lighthouse and city figure for the overall complex rose to $4.5 million.

Dedication of the new Seattle Lighthouse home took place on April 3, 1967. The featured speaker was Robert C. Goodpasture, vice president and general manager of the National Industries for the Blind (NIB), New York. Seattle Mayor J. Dorm Braman also spoke. (When a second-floor addition was being built in January 1969, a heavy windstorm blew 100 feet of a framed plywood wall not yet tied together with ceiling joists onto Plum Street and a parked car. A frightened witness described the event as like "an earthquake.")

Funds to build the new Plum Street facility came in part from the sale ($45,000) of the Seattle Lighthouse building on Elliott Avenue. Bequests to the Lighthouse in the form of properties also contributed to the budget. The combination was an important example of how charitable giving and philanthropy can make a difference. Rudy Elmer, who oversaw the transition, proudly stated that no monies from charitable organizations were used to construct the new quarters.

The revitalized Lighthouse survived a contentious and sometimes confusing decade—the infamous 1960s. Seattle's Century 21, the Seattle World's Fair, had an exciting 1962 run. President John F. Kennedy was assassinated in Dallas, Texas, on November 22, 1963. The battle for civil rights was under way. In 1964, the Gulf of Tonkin incident occurred, driving the United States further into what would be called the Vietnam War. Protest singers Joan Baez and Bob Dylan were popular. Polyester, bell-bottom trousers, and miniskirts were the rage. The Richard M. Nixon administration and Watergate were on the horizon. Despite these daunting and sometimes strange times, the Seattle Lighthouse resolutely moved forward.

The question of "profit" was occasionally raised in regard to nonprofit organizations such as the Lighthouse. According to attorney and board member Ray Haman, an excess of operating revenue over expense is necessary to survive. Enough money must be on hand or anticipated for research and development to sustain viability during economic downturns, to recover from failed ventures, and for the purchase of high-tech equipment (a necessity for blind employees at the Lighthouse). In sum, Haman points out that the Seattle Lighthouse is successful "because it pursues its charitable objective in a businesslike manner."

Under the "new" management, with Rudy Elmer at the helm, assisted by Hank Nakagawa, and later under the management of George Jacobson, the Seattle Lighthouse took a closer look at the federal government as a prospective customer for company products. Over the next several decades military neckties, signal pennants, canteens and canteen caps, easels, and business cards, among other items, were designed and manufactured at the Lighthouse, under demanding government specifications.

Paul Fletcher, Lighthouse quality manager, noted that the easel program began in the early 1970s and inspired confidence in "cross-selling," that is, finding buyers in both the government and private sectors. In fact, easels were one of the first products made under the JWOD Act (see Chapter 4). Today, two basic easels are produced, one with

*George "Jake" Jacobson,
Lighthouse president
since 1979*

a white dry-erase board
and the other with the traditional green chalkboard.

Other steps into the age
of technology and manu-
facturing (see Chapter 8)
included the installation of
machines for a new Injec-
tion Mold Department. Also, computer-paper and hang-
ing-file-folder projects were undertaken. The famous
patented Anglematic Mop, designed by Lighthouse
employees in 1983, is now sold to both the government
and the general public. High-visibility traffic safety vests,
helmets, and armbands are manufactured for the General
Services Administration for redistribution to the armed
forces and sold to other organizations.

Looking farther down the road, and representative of
U.S. concern with homeland security, the Lighthouse is
developing a capacity to manufacture backpack hydra-
tion systems, so that first responders such as firefighters
and police can have safe supplies of drinking water during emergencies.

Lighthouse management took an essential step when
it paid increased attention to the manufacturing process.
Lighthouse products were competing with those made

by commercial outlets across the country and, as board member Fred Mendoza stated, the company had to build a "better mousetrap."

Expertise in training and technology is constantly being enhanced. For example, adult computer education courses provide general computer knowledge, while the service office systems build upon computer applications used in customer-service skills.

Like any other manufacturer competing in today's marketplace, the Seattle Lighthouse realizes that employee training plays an essential role. Therefore, training remains an integral part of the Lighthouse commitment to providing blind employees with support necessary for success in the workplace. Blind, Deaf-Blind, and develop-

Warehouse operation (1970s). Mop heads were sold to the federal government under the Javits-Wagner-O'Day Act.

mentally disabled blind employees take advantage of job coaching, orientation, and mobility instruction. They also look for opportunities to advance their computer and adaptive technology skills, reading Braille and using American Sign Language (ASL). Further, machine-shop employees acquire new skills and learn new jobs through an innovative peer training program.

Other employee opportunities and in-house training opportunities include beginning computer skills, a screen-magnifying program (ZoomText), screen readers with voice synthesizers, advanced e-mail and keyboarding, reading work orders in Braille, and ASL courses.

In 2002, federal monies allowed the Lighthouse to initiate a pilot program to improve technology in the lives of people who are Deaf-Blind. Necessary skills for this new program are learned in the Lighthouse Technology Training Center.

The Lighthouse has been pleased to host interns as part of the state of Washington Youth Employment Solutions (YES) program. This program places blind students, ages sixteen to twenty-one, in paid work situations during the summer, as well as providing an independent living experience. Students from around the state typically spend six weeks living in a rented University of Washington sorority house, traveling throughout the city using public transportation, shopping for groceries, preparing meals, and earning their first paychecks from employers like the Lighthouse.

To enhance and increase employee confidence and opportunities, the Group Supported Employment (GSE)

Program was introduced in the 1970s. Its central purpose is to provide employee "inclusion" in all aspects of Lighthouse work, and it is designed for blind or Deaf-Blind individuals with significant disabilities such as autism. The GSE Program focuses on getting employees "ready for work" and supports Lighthouse workers in virtually every department.

The above summary of highlights attempts to show the upward and outward progress made by the Seattle Lighthouse since its 1964 merger with Handcrest. These changes and new programs—really a quantum jump—have resulted in a manufacturing and training organization that has soared beyond its long-ago and antiquated description as a "sheltered workshop."

In line with these changes and programs is the emergence of a new, brief, right-to-the-point Seattle Lighthouse mission statement: "To

Quincy Daniels cuts aluminum stock for ladders sold to federal customers under the Javits-Wagner-O'Day Act (1980s).
Photo courtesy of Jim Bates Photography

create and enhance opportunities for independence and self-sufficiency of people who are blind, Deaf-Blind and blind with other disabilities."

CHAPTER 7
On Hood Canal

How best the yoke of silence
Can my spirit bear?
What work to do while waiting?
What talents left to share.

Meanwhile, I'll use my hands like lightning
And transform the silence borne,
Into signs with new meaning, brightening
The darkness of fear into a new form.

By Edna Shipley-Conner
from the poem "On My Impending Deafness"

Hood Canal is an eighty-mile-long tidal channel on the eastern rim of the wild and mountainous Olympic Peninsula in Washington state. Originally named "Hood's Channel" by Captain George Vancouver in May 1792 for his boss, Lord (and admiral) Samuel Hood, this fishhook-shaped fjord is a slow-flushing protein factory stocked with clams, mussels, salmon, and world-famous oysters.

U.S. Highway 101, which evolved from Indian trails,

follows a thirty-seven-mile serpentine path along the canal's west shore. Small towns—Duckabush, Hamma Hamma, Lilliwaup, Brinnon, and Quilcene, each of them famous for oyster beds—line this scenic route.

On Hood Canal's eastern shore, not far from the Navy port of Bremerton, is a settlement called Seabeck. Pioneer Marshall Blinn named this scenic community for a town in Maine. Blinn, who also invested in Seattle real estate, established a sawmill on this site in 1857. In recent times, the major attraction of the community has been a 700-acre church conference campus. The Seattle Lighthouse for the Blind has for years used the grounds, known as the Seabeck Conference Center, to host one of the nation's most unusual gatherings—the annual Deaf-Blind Retreat.

In August 2003, the Deaf-Blind Retreat celebrated its twenty-fifth anniversary. The Lighthouse is proud to have conceived and hosted what has become an internationally recognized event for Deaf-Blind people. The Lighthouse's role in the retreat emanates from its experience as a major employer of individuals who are Deaf-Blind, dating to 1969.

Retreat beginnings were modest—a friendly letter from Stephen Ehrlich, who was Deaf-Blind, and taught Deaf-Blind persons at the Seattle Lighthouse. Ehrlich's June 26, 1978, invitation to "Friends and Volunteers" to join a "camp program" for Deaf-Blind adults inaugurated what became a major event for Deaf-Blind participants. The 1978 fee was $50 (in 2003 it was $260), and the camp took place at the Red Barn Ranch in Auburn, Washington.

*Volunteer Brogan Thomsen and a Deaf-Blind retreat
attendee prepare for a wild jet-ski ride at Hood Canal,
Washington (2000).*

The first budget included costs for a nurse, a lifeguard, table games, insurance, transportation, and "parties."

Twelve Deaf-Blind campers, including seven from out of state, were welcomed to the inaugural event. Also participating were sixteen volunteers, seven of them deaf. Remarkably, many of the original participants and volunteers have remained in touch with the Seattle Lighthouse, and occasionally revisit retreats.

The Deaf-Blind Retreat arose from an interesting environment. The city of Seattle attracts many Deaf-Blind people because it is the home of what may be the nation's best regional Deaf-Blind support system. There are more Deaf-Blind people in, for example, Los Angeles, but only Seattle has an impressive array of Deaf-Blind services.

Besides the Lighthouse, other Seattle-area agencies

offering services to Deaf-Blind community members include the Deaf-Blind Service Center, Washington State Deaf-Blind Citizens, Abused Deaf Women's Advocacy Services, the Washington State Program for Deaf-Blind Children, and the Helen Keller National Center Regional Office.

Nationally, very few schools or agencies provide effective support to Deaf-Blind persons, leaving many without basic education, work, or social and cultural opportunities. The Seattle Lighthouse creates such opportunities. Deaf-Blind Retreats are therefore a natural and appropriate step for the Lighthouse in providing an environment leading to the independence of Deaf-Blind persons.

The original Deaf-Blind Retreat (1978) at the Red Barn Ranch, Auburn, Washington

Perhaps the largest employer of Deaf-Blind persons in the country—maybe in the world—Seattle Lighthouse has a staff fluent in American Sign Language (ASL) as well as other types of sign language and communication skills. Offering competitive wages and benefits, vocational-technical training, and full or part-time jobs, the Lighthouse is well known to Deaf-Blind persons everywhere.

In 2003, the Lighthouse reissued the Deaf-Blind Retreat mission statement:

"The purpose of the Deaf-Blind Retreat is to give Deaf-Blind persons an opportunity to engage in peer support, networking, recreational and educational activities in a completely accessible environment. Deaf-Blind persons plan and coordinate activities working with a team. Attendance is open to Deaf-Blind persons nationally and from other countries."

Details of Deaf-Blind camps/retreats make an interesting contrast with camping experiences familiar to sighted readers.

Participants at the first camp—who, keep in mind, were Deaf-Blind or had other disabilities—rode horses, swam and played in the swimming pool, picked strawberries, went on local tours, and engaged in what was described as "talk, talk, talk." Each attendee made her or his own choices about activities.

In 1982, the retreat moved to Pilgrim Firs near Port Orchard, Washington (not far from Seabeck), on the Kitsap Peninsula. A nearby lake offered fishing, and a hot tub was available. Other activities included the construction of an Indian sweat lodge, participation in a drama workshop, tai chi sessions, folding origami cranes, and enjoying fireworks on the Fourth of July. Pilgrim Firs saw the first "rope" trail system set up to allow Deaf-Blind attendees to move independently about the camp.

The early camps were opportunities to experience group communications for Deaf-Blind people who lived in other states and did not have much contact with other Deaf-Blind individuals. Those who were used to one-on-one contact now had opportunities to join group conversations, listen to what others were saying, and brainstorm together. Around-the-clock availability was a challenge, and the skills of many novice student interpreters were stretched.

Later, Hood Canal's Seabeck Retreats became so successful (172 participants in 1988, 175 in 2003), with the good word spreading among participants and related organizations, that many Deaf-Blind persons moved to the Seattle area. Volunteers and Deaf-Blind participants came from out of state (especially Louisiana, California, and Texas), Canada, and overseas (over the years participants have traveled from Switzerland, Germany, Great Britain, Australia, New Zealand, Finland, Denmark, Hong Kong, and Israel).

After evaluating the busy Seabeck retreats for several years, the Seattle Lighthouse introduced several changes, including:

1. Carefully choosing "qualified" volunteers.
2. Improving transportation.

3. Improving accessibility, with an extended "rope" guiding system and reflective tape; camp materials in accessible formats such as Braille and large print; and cell phones, pagers, and walkie-talkies.

4. Expanding the Deaf-Blind program staff.

5. Developing interesting workshops—for example, hosting sessions on cultural diversity, baking/cooking, and AIDS/HIV.

6. Introducing a richer arts and crafts program.

7. Organizing more outdoor activities, such as jet skiing, surf biking, kayaking, and paddle-boating.

8. Teaching and using advanced technology—for example, travel equipment, the Internet, and Braille captioning.

9. Scheduling a variety of dances.

10. Offering programs about self-care, such as massage, facials, and haircuts.

11. Introducing or expanding fitness classes such as yoga, tai chi, biking, and rock-wall climbing.

12. Introducing "just plain fun" and entertainment activities including mazes, chess, and a tactile Pictionary.

After the mid-1980s, and with clear memories of occasional cool or rainy June weather, organizers moved the retreats to late August. The later date sometimes conflicted with the schedules of volunteer-interpreters who had to return to school or because of Labor Day weekend, but the extra sunshine made the change worthwhile.

Eligibility to attend retreats is as follows: " . . . attendees must be Deaf-Blind or legally blind and either deaf, significantly hard of hearing or late deafened." The retreats are for Deaf-Blind adults "who are able to make independent decisions" and are 18 years or older. Sixteen-year-olds are sometimes welcome if they are attending with a parent or adult friend.

Volunteer-interpreters, both deaf and hearing, must have experience guiding and communicating with Deaf-Blind people. Participants must have an acceptable level of fluency in ASL.

The retreat-participant selection process was shaped by experience. Safety issues are paramount, and applications received by the postmarked deadline are given priority. Another factor is trying to have a "balanced" retreat—for example, matching Deaf-Blind persons who use ASL with peers who also use ASL.

Every effort is made to ensure that retreats are affordable and inclusive. To support those efforts, partial scholarships are available. However, participants must pay for their own transportation to and from the retreat. Retreat fees cover only a portion of expenses. Contributions from foundations, corporations, local businesses, and individuals complement the budget.

After twenty-five years, the retreat has become successful for many reasons: the delightful location(s); the low cost; its reputation as a week of "relaxation, support and fun"; and the enthusiastic cadre of qualified volunteer-interpreters.

Paula Hoffman, director of rehabilitation services at the Lighthouse, who has helped organize and evaluate the retreats for years, points out that since 1989 the retreats have a ratio of 1.5 volunteer-interpreters to each Deaf-

Blind participant. Hoffman and the Lighthouse team make a conscious effort to "take good care" of volunteer-interpreters so that they will enjoy the experience, have occasional breaks, and return to future retreats.

The extraordinary retreat experience has found a firm place on the Seattle Lighthouse calendar. Staffing, fundraising, volunteer training, promotion, and management of these events have long been in place.

Visitors and friends are invited to see for themselves by contacting The Lighthouse for the Blind, Inc., or by visiting (www.deafblindlh.org). Information is available, and contributions in many forms are welcome!

Perhaps it's time to take a new and different look at Captain Vancouver's shimmering Hood Canal.

CHAPTER 8
Hardware & Software

Did it all begin with the Industrial Revolution, usually associated with England from 1750 to 1850? Maybe so, but the world of technology in the current millennium is an extraordinary leap forward from the steam engine, electrical power, and railroads of yesteryear.

The Lighthouse for the Blind is riding the crest of new ideas and technology that have opened opportunities beyond anyone's imagination for people who are blind, Deaf-Blind, and others with multiple disabilities.

Technology at the Seattle Lighthouse is constantly monitored, because technological change and modification occur almost weekly in the wider world. Consequently, people who are blind and have other disabilities are able to do things today that seemed impossible a few years ago. As computers get smaller and faster, career opportunities expand. The Lighthouse analyzes those opportunities and then creates a product or service at a fair market price.

For example, blind and other disabled Lighthouse employees can set up their own jobs and interact with machines that "talk." Some of these machines are called Computer Numerically Controlled (CNC). These

Mary Helen Scheiber prepares Nike water-bottle grips for shipping.

machines are technologically beneficial to all in manufacturing. At the Lighthouse they allow blind people to independently set up their own jobs, while at the same time solving customer requests for small job runs and more frequent deliveries.

The Internet—used by blind people at home and at work—stimulates the development of new products. The Internet also allows direct contact with customers and complements traditional direct-marketing efforts. The Internet brings to the Lighthouse an opportunity to take its manufacturing strength and develop new niche markets.

For approximately $17,000 (in 2004) a workstation can be installed for blind people to perform the duties of a customer service representative. Bob Johnson, Lighthouse vice president for sales and marketing, confirmed that "these new, technologically advanced workstations help keep Lighthouse employees in the market and competitive with sighted organizations." Johnson noted that technology has not only leveled the playing field for people who are blind, but has worked to create advantages in the marketplace. Customer service representative jobs are examples of technology creating new Lighthouse opportunities.

Deaf-Blind teaching and technology services manager Amy Koehl directs a federally funded pilot program that places specially adapted computer equipment in the homes of selected Deaf-Blind individuals. Those who receive this help must have basic computer skills and knowledge of Braille. Candidates for the program are evaluated by the Technology Training Center (TTC) staff, and must indicate that they have a practical need for the equipment and a clean, safe place in which to work.

Koehl also oversees job training and orientation activities collectively called Group Supported Employment (GSE), a program for people who are blind or Deaf-Blind and live with an additional developmental disability. GSE teaches job skills and production-line work and assists in integrating participants with their coworkers. The program's purpose is to provide support and training that enable employees to succeed. The range of support varies. For example, some employees require more accommodation than others due to individual disabilities. Other GSE features include positive social interaction with coworkers, training to live independently, and successful communication. The GSE program represents a successful effort to reach out to all blind and visually impaired people, regardless of their other disabilities.

Paul Fletcher, quality control manager, is responsible for the Seattle Lighthouse's adoption of the ISO Quality System. Qualification of the Lighthouse under this international quality standard came as a requirement of the Boeing contract, and was achieved with Boeing's direct support and assistance. Many Seattle Lighthouse employees were involved in meeting this rigorous standard. Achieving this goal is illustrative of the Lighthouse as a world-class manufacturer.

Across the nation, agencies employing people who are blind have traditionally provided manufacturing jobs, but they have not uniformly emphasized rehabilitation programs. Conversely, the Lighthouse, beginning with its 1914 production and marketing of crafts, and continuing with the Boeing contracts and the Javits-Wagner-O'Day (JWOD) program, has developed a broad and comprehensive rehabilitation effort. Both halves of the Lighthouse—manufacturing and rehabilitation—hold national significance in the field of blindness.

From making place mats, wicker baskets, and brooms to creating machine-shop jobs, the Seattle Lighthouse has created meaningful employment for blind and disabled persons, and, in the last couple of decades, for Deaf-Blind persons. Those jobs have resulted in the production of useful general consumer or military items. Still, the Lighthouse constantly investigates ways to build a "better mousetrap." Technology is often the answer. Despite the Lighthouse's emphasis on jobs, training, and independent living, a collateral rehabilitation program has always been present.

By providing high-quality, accessible jobs, the Seattle Lighthouse creates opportunities for blind people. However, a job is often not enough. Lighthouse rehabilitation programs provide the vocational and living skills, training, and special support necessary for true independence.

Boeing aircraft parts were manufactured by Handcrest

(and, later, Lighthouse) employees beginning in 1951, including small aluminum clips for the KC-97 Stratocruiser (see Chapter 5). Perhaps Boeing milling machines were a technological breakthrough at the Seattle Lighthouse?

The Boeing Company also invested time and money in training workers for jobs. According to Don Helsel, Lighthouse director of manufacturing, Boeing helped diversify the workshop and created new employee skills and knowledge. Both parties—Boeing and the Lighthouse—have been pleased with their contracts, which in fact have pointed the way to the manufacture of new products. To this day (after more than fifty years) that relationship has prospered.

The Seattle Lighthouse's Boeing Department features relatively new CNC manufacturing equipment. This state-of-the-art technology, including press brakes and routers, allows an operator to program several jobs at one time. These machines are able to make one form and then readjust to make two or three more. In the past, those readjustments were done manually.

Roosevelt Stevenson, National Industries for the Blind Employee of the Year in 1999, operates a vertical milling machine in the manufacture of aircraft parts for The Boeing Company.

Boeing has put generous resources into improving the Lighthouse machine shop and has supported training programs that strive to raise the skill level of employees, increase math and problem-solving skills, and provide computer lab time for individual study. The payoff is better-made, more sophisticated Boeing parts produced by skilled workers. (It should be added that besides turning out quality products by trained employees, machinists are alert to shop safety, a foremost concern.)

Boeing contracts virtually created the Handcrest/Lighthouse machine shop more than fifty years ago. Today's machine-shop employees operate equipment ranging from hand tools to advanced CNC machine centers. The Lighthouse machine shop differs from other machine shops in only one way: it has modifications for accessibility. In 2000, Lighthouse employee Jim Smith became the first blind person in the world to be trained and certified to operate a CNC machine.

With training, including an emphasis on safety, machine-shop operators turn out parts that are more than 99.97 percent within requirements. In fact, that is the percentage of acceptable parts the Lighthouse supplies to Boeing on average. This level of performance has resulted in the Lighthouse twice receiving Boeing's Q100 Club award for exceptional quality performance as a supplier.

Former employee Margarita Eng, who was once nominated for Seattle Lighthouse Worker of the Year, held a job in the Boeing machine shop during the 1970s and early 1980s. She did not always understand the use of each part she helped make, but that circumstance didn't slow her enthusiasm for the job at hand. Today the Lighthouse uses a wide variety of employee committees, regular employee meetings, and other participatory approaches that keep workers informed and involved in business operations.

After a 1953 "cold call" on PACCAR, the Bellevue, Washington, manufacturer of trucks, Handcrest manager Rudy Elmer was pleased to see a new contract emerge. Handcrest employees were soon cutting holes in plywood for PACCAR refrigeration cars.

Sewing was once a major activity at the Lighthouse. The Sewing Department produced military neckties, signal pennants, and sleeping bags, among other items.

Following the 1964 merger of the Seattle Lighthouse and Handcrest (see Chapter 6), manufacturing took on new life. Traditional and familiar Lighthouse crafts began to dwindle in number as Handcrest manufacturing moved into technological fields.

In 1970, safety guards were installed on Lighthouse stamping presses. The guards' sensing elements set up a "light curtain" around the work area. If an operator's hand or finger penetrates this "curtain," the machine stops.

Seattle Lighthouse employee Gina Lewis, who is blind, recalls bagging brooms as a summer student in 1973. With the introduction of canteens and a canteen valve assembly in the 1980s, new opportunities appeared for her and other employees. With training and experience Lewis has been able to move from job to job, each time accumulating additional skills.

Lewis noted that some air-driven machinery (technology has many faces) created uncomfortable noise levels. That circumstance can be especially disconcerting for blind employees used to relying on their hearing for information and orientation.

The Seattle Lighthouse has met the needs of workers within noisy areas by using "noise-limiting" headphones. These headphones reduce the noise level, but also utilize computerized technology, thereby permitting employees to easily hear spoken words.

Injection molding was introduced in the early 1980s. That process injects hot plastic into a mold, which is then cooled, and the desired part is created. Examples of injection-molded products include paper-trimmer parts, mop heads, utensils, and postage-stamp trays. Molding machines opened the door to a new family of products. Six different machines are used in the injection-molding process.

Among the most successful injection-molding items are components for canteens and canteen caps that the Lighthouse manufactures for the U.S. Armed Forces. The canteen caps are unique in that they permit canteens to be used by servicemen and -women when they wear gas masks. Each of these caps is individually tested at the Lighthouse. These products are another example of Lighthouse's capability to produce technological products that meet the highest quality standards.

JWOD, the law of the land, resulted in many new opportunities (noted above). The late Rear Admiral W.R. "Wally" Dowd, Jr., former longtime chairman of the

Lighthouse board, supported the JWOD program in his position as chief of the Naval Supply Corporation and in his long service on the President's Committee of Purchase from People Who are Blind or Severely Disabled. Vice president of sales and marketing Bob Johnson and others recall Dowd's knowledge of the federal marketplace and his support and guidance of Lighthouse management. Johnson especially remembers Dowd's dedication to seeking independence and opportunity for Lighthouse employees who are blind, visually impaired, or have multiple disabilities.

Rear Admiral Wallace R. Dowd, Jr., chairman of the board of trustees from 1980 through 1999

Easels were among the early products made at the Lighthouse under the JWOD Act. The first aluminum easel design came from the General Services Administration (GSA), but it was redesigned fifteen years later by Lighthouse employees. In 2003, Don Helsel, Lighthouse director of manufacturing, noted that easel production "accounts for five full-time jobs for blind and Deaf-Blind employees at the Seattle Lighthouse."

Another JWOD product line is high-visibility traffic safety vests. In 2004, approximately 1,500 vests were sold each month to the GSA for distribution to branches of the armed forces. Production supervisor Jerry Kopp pointed out that the Lighthouse also offers a line of JWOD general-purpose safety vests, which were originally developed by the Lighthouse for sale to the Pacific Northwest Bell Telephone Company.

Another popular Lighthouse product is the famous, patented Anglematic Mop. Designed to meet different needs with its adjustable head, the Anglematic Mop is known throughout the country.

Not every Lighthouse investment has been a resounding success. The National Industries for the Blind (NIB) urged Seattle Lighthouse to manufacture computer paper. A sophisticated paper machine was purchased in 1991 and installed for $600,000. After several years of successful production, the machine was sold in the late 1990s when federal government demand for that paper declined.

Near the bustling canteen and easel assembly areas, one can find the busy Stamp Department. Beginning in the late 1990s, new positions were created to manufacture an array of stamps for the U.S. Postal Service and private companies. When you see ready-made stamps that say "FIRST CLASS" or "PAID," they may have been manufactured at the Lighthouse for the Blind.

In addition to stamps, the Lighthouse Custom Business Products line includes award certificates, plaques, and laser-engraved wooden desk accessories. Additional items in the line include business cards, writing instruments, notepads, binders, conference kits, and more. In the case of business cards and several other products, the customer, using the Internet, can be directly involved in design and content.

The Lighthouse offers two computer-training courses for working-age adults who are blind. Adult computer education, the first component, focuses on general computer knowledge, specific adaptive technologies, and an introduction to résumé writing and job interviews. The second set of classes, service office systems, builds upon the first, dealing more specifically with customer-service skills and the computer applications used in that field. Vocational counselors from the Washington State Department of Services for the Blind refer students to the Light-

Dana Marmion, customer service representative for custom business products sold to federal agencies under the Javits-Wagner-O'Day Act.

house. The program serves between eighty-five and a hundred blind people from Washington state annually.

Over the past ten years, the Lighthouse has provided this comprehensive computer and customer-service training to hundreds of blind and visually impaired individuals. Nine months in duration, the courses take students from basic keyboarding to mastery of standard Microsoft Office applications such as Outlook, Word, Access, and Excel. Concurrent with these lessons, students learn how to utilize adaptive technologies that are best suited to them, such as screen magnification, speech output, Braille displays, or a combination of the three. These are the primary types of adaptive technology that make a job in today's computerized workplace accessible for someone who is blind.

In further support of technological advances, the Seattle Lighthouse has established a variety of other training programs. For example, computer instruction is provided in either visual or tactile sign language.

American Sign Language is defined as a "visual foreign language, distinct from English." Tactile Sign Language involves the placement of one's hands over another person's hands when forming signs. Additional programs train ASL interpreters and teach people Braille.

Additional training has been offered over the years. For example, the Deaf-Blind program has made formal internship positions available for sign-language-interpreting students, as well as myriad opportunities. Deaf-Blind community classes, sponsored by the Seattle Lighthouse, are offered at Seattle Central Community College. These classes give Deaf-Blind students unique opportunities to acquire information about topics of their choice. Many students attend these classes to gain knowledge and skills; others come for "social aspects"—i.e., to get out of an isolated existence experienced by many Deaf-Blind persons.

George Jacobson, president of the Lighthouse for the Blind, wrote in the house newsletter *Horizons* (2000), "Adaptive computer technology and e-commerce via the Web will allow creation of jobs that blind people could not have dreamed of . . . just a decade ago." He added

Deaf-Blind employee Jenné Arnold accepts the National Industries for the Blind 2003 Employee of the Year award.

that in the near future blind and visually impaired employees "will participate in every aspect of our operation."

Not missing an opportunity, and as a result of burgeoning technology, the Lighthouse is developing online shopping for its customers. At present, testing is complete and the first orders have been received. Federal government agencies can use online shopping to order business cards. This system lets customers see what their business cards will look like before they place an order. Additional online ordering systems are planned.

Lighthouse board members and employees invite visitors to see for themselves "Seattle's best-kept secret." The lessons are exciting: technology, training, and enlightened management have created jobs for blind, Deaf-Blind, and other people with multiple disabilities. Call the Lighthouse to join a tour of its remarkable facility.

Another way to keep up with technology—and many other Lighthouse matters—is to ask for a free subscription to *Horizons*, the Lighthouse newsletter. Call 206 436 2110 or send a request via e-mail to (information@seattlelh.org).

CHAPTER 9
From Broomcorn to New Horizons

Gazing into crystal balls and reading tea leaves are the wonderful stuff of legend, but the Lighthouse for the Blind takes prognostication in a different direction.

Ninety years of Lighthouse experience has contributed to a rich storehouse of business, cultural, and social data. The history of the Lighthouse, which has been influenced by internal and external events and by individuals, clearly points to bold and interesting future opportunities.

Creating jobs for people who are blind, Deaf-Blind, and have other disabilities is and always has been the Lighthouse's primary focus. Steps to achieve the creation of steady, high-quality jobs for blind people include developing new products, improving existing products, and modernizing production lines. Although this sounds similar to goals endorsed by other manufacturing and training organizations, there is a significant difference. The Lighthouse constantly strives to ensure that jobs throughout the organization as well as opportunities for advancement and all training programs are completely accessible for people who are blind and Deaf-Blind. That mission requires constant attention to the latest innova-

High-quality brooms were a mainstay of job creation at the Seattle Lighthouse in the early decades.

tions in training, adaptive technology, and communications methods.

Broomcorn, mentioned in this chapter's title, was the raw material—obtained from Kansas and Washington state—used in the manufacture of brooms. That sturdy and famous product was the virtual symbol of the Lighthouse for almost sixty years. Employees designed, made, bundled, delivered (to specialty outlets), and sold (usually door-to-door) the finest-quality brooms ever known in the Pacific Northwest and beyond. "Look for the Lighthouse label" was once a familiar marketing slogan—and brooms led the way.

Many interesting stories about Lighthouse brooms survive, but George Bailey's tale is notable. Bailey sold brooms after graduating from the University of

Washington School of Music. He was also hired to play the chimes in the university's wooden chimes tower. He had been playing the chimes for thirty-two years, three times daily, when a fire broke out in the tower on Sunday morning, May 24, 1949.

At first, many believed that George had perished in the blaze, but he was found at home getting ready for his Sunday concert. Raymond B. Allen, president of the university, assured George that new chimes would quickly be installed in the music building—sixty-one Flemish and twenty-five English bells—and that his job was secure. The sometime broom salesman resumed his campus music performances within a few weeks. The last surviving bell from the fire was dedicated in 1952, George Bailey attending, at Seattle's Washelli cemetery.

Another "broom" story involves Don Donaldson. Donaldson and another blind companion (each of them coincidentally blinded by separate dynamite explosions) toured Washington state while students at the University of Washington in the 1930s. The driver they hired stole all the funds collected from broom sales, leaving them stranded in Bellingham, Washington. They immediately reported the incident, assuring the Lighthouse that they would pay back every penny.

While discussing this disaster at the Seattle Lighthouse, Donaldson asked if someone could recommend a local ophthalmologist. Don got a name, saw the doctor, and his sight in one eye was restored. His later career included many years as teacher and principal at the Vancouver School for the Blind. Donaldson tells more stories in his 2004 autobiography, *What's in a Name* (see the Bibliography).

Leaving brooms far behind, in the coming years computerization and automation will determine most Lighthouse jobs, many of them Web-based. And manufacturing and product sales will be the core of tomorrow's Lighthouse financial statements.

Lighthouse training is constantly being upgraded, with emphasis on a more sophisticated work environment. Adaptive equipment such as Braille displays and speech synthesizers will be widespread.

The Deaf-Blind community is now an integral part of Lighthouse activities and will become more important in the future. It is anticipated that the wider community will increasingly turn to the Seattle Lighthouse for expertise, training, and technical assistance.

Another trend is the upward mobility of blind employees to achieve supervisory and management positions. The Lighthouse is also committed to assisting blind, visually impaired, and Deaf-Blind employees in moving into the private sector if they so choose. Facing a very narrow range of options, seven out of ten blind adults are still not in the workforce.

Stretching from a small downtown Seattle craft shop and Association for the Blind in 1914, to a twenty-first-century manufacturing center on Plum Street, Seattle Lighthouse has experienced ninety years of progress and growth. External events, such as economic depressions, foreign wars, the spectacular rise of Boeing, the 1964

*Jim Smith operates a computer numerically controlled milling
machine outfitted with a screen-reading speech synthesizer.*

Lighthouse merger with Handcrest, changing board
leadership, and the introduction of computer technology, have swiftly and inexorably advanced Lighthouse
programs.

Looking ahead has always been a Lighthouse responsibility. For example, in 2003 the Lighthouse leadership
team undertook a comprehensive strategic planning
process. The team identified five main areas for the next
phase of Lighthouse history:

1. Maximizing effectiveness of job creation and revenue
generation through business activities.
2. Establishing a consistent presence and effective e-commerce distribution channels on the Worldwide Web.

3. Effectively utilizing information technology to further the Lighthouse mission and activities.

4. To enhance human resources and training programs and policies.

5. To create a comprehensive public relations and resource development program.

A primary focus of this last goal is to inform the general public about the mission and activities of the Lighthouse as well as the capability of blind and Deaf-Blind people to live independent and self-sufficient lives. The book you hold in your hand is a direct result of this commitment by both board and staff to make sure The Lighthouse for the Blind, Inc., is no longer "Seattle's best-kept secret."

Lighthouse employees enjoy a summer event in the
Ethel L. Dupar Fragrant Garden (2003).

The Seattle Lighthouse has employee and visitor amenities similar to those of other manufacturing organizations, with a couple of unusual exceptions.

On the south side of the Lighthouse building is a relaxing patch of shrubbery, flowers, and rare plants. The Ethel L. Dupar Fragrant Garden, established in 1973 through the generosity of Mrs. Dupar, is presently undergoing a revival under the green thumb of master gardener Helen Weber and a host of volunteers. In 2004, the Dupar family decided to provide an annual donation to the garden, leading to complete restoration of the original site within two years. A plaque in the garden reads:

> *"The kiss of the sun for pardon,*
> *The song of the birds for mirth,*
> *One is nearer God's heart in a garden*
> *Than anywhere else on earth."*

Tours of the garden are welcomed. More information is available from the Lighthouse Public Relations and Resource Development Department, 206 436 2110, or by e-mail to (information@seattlelh.org).

Another unique Lighthouse amenity is a well-ventilated, state-of-the-art guide dog facility. Built in 1988, and located next to the Ethel L. Dupar Fragrant Garden, the cinder-block kennel has twenty-five stalls. Clem Provatakis, Lighthouse facilities manager, recalled that at first there were problems obtaining a Seattle permit because "dog kennels" are not allowed within city limits. After affirming that dogs would not be spending the

Deaf-Blind employee Lillian Meske receives computer instruction from Bruce Visser in the Deaf-Blind Technology and Training Center.

night in the facility, the city issued a permit.

On average about eight to twelve dogs use the facility each week. The rectangular structure is disinfected weekly by custodial staff. Exhaust fans and louvered windows are used for air circulation. Radiant heat provides a comfortable winter environment. Guide dogs are welcome in administrative areas of the Lighthouse, and several employees keep their companions nearby. However, "dogs and machine shops just don't mix," according to Provatakis. High-pitched noises and the possibility of flying chips could be confusing and dangerous to a service animal.

The Lighthouse notes that there has been a recent increase in the use of guide dogs by Deaf-Blind people. Those dogs are trained to respond to visual signals and sign language, rather than to audio or voice commands. Deaf-Blind guide dog users have formed a group that includes members of the wider community. Costs of sign-language interpreters needed at their meetings are covered through a federal appropriation.

The Lighthouse for the Blind is bullish about the future and invites you to take a closer look. Remember, it is "Seattle's best-kept secret."

The following vision of tomorrow, which concludes this chapter, was written by George Jacobson, president of The Lighthouse for the Blind, Inc.

WE ARE ABOUT CHOICE

When I imagine the future of the Puget Sound region I see a community that has been positively affected by the Seattle Lighthouse, a community of employers and workplaces where people who are blind and Deaf-Blind are an integral part of the economy.

I also imagine a community where it is commonplace to see blind and visually impaired people working at all sorts of jobs. Where young blind people have the same opportunities as their sighted classmates to land the first summer and after-school jobs. A community where blind professionals with advanced degrees are holding the same positions as their sighted peers and where seeing computers with Braille displays and speech programs in offices and computer labs are no longer unusual events.

On the surface, this vision might seem easily attainable, but the reality of unemployment statistics and ever-present poverty tells us we have a long road to travel. According to the National Organization on Disability, more than seventy percent of adults with severe disabilities are not in the workforce. This compares to thirty-three percent of the non-disabled population. Only one in ten adults with severe disabilities own their own home, compared with seven out of ten persons without disabilities. More than one-third of adults with severe disabilities are living below the poverty line. If we focused solely on Americans who are Deaf-Blind, these disparities would be even more alarming.

The most disturbing thing about the above statistics is that they have not changed appreciably over time. The rate of unemployment for blind adults has remained near seventy percent for decades, both before and after passage of the Americans with Disabilities Act (1992).

I believe the main reasons these problems persist can be found in our society's attitudes towards individuals who are blind. Polls indicate that fear of blindness is one of the top three concerns of many people. People who are sighted, and have not learned to live with visual impairment, cannot imagine what their lives would be like if they could not see.

For example, a typical employer interviewing a blind job candidate might think, "How in the world would he (or she) function as a receptionist?" "How could they file?" "Use the computer?" "Dial the telephone"? These are natural reactions by someone who isn't familiar with how blind people function. There are blindness skills that adults with visual impairments learn, allowing them to live and work successfully and efficiently. Because of a lack of understanding in the larger society, people who are blind must overcome stereotypes, myths, and discrimination when seeking employment. Employers who make a commitment to learn about blindness and available adaptive technology can do a great deal to change our community's perceptions about blind people.

The best way the Seattle Lighthouse can help other

employers who are committed to leveling the playing field for blind people is by showcasing examples of successful blind employees. The Lighthouse for the Blind, Inc., is a successful manufacturing company, committed to creating jobs throughout an organization that is accessible to blind people. This means insuring that appropriate training, technology, and systems of accommodation are in place. We also can show other employers what that training, technology, and support can look like.

Some examples:

* By fitting electronic calipers with a simple and inexpensive voice synthesizer, a blind machinist can measure parts.
* By using a scanner and special software a visually impaired receptionist can scan the mail and read it with screen magnification.
* A blind customer-service representative can access customer databases and fill out order forms using a computer equipped with a Braille display.
* A brief orientation session will allow a new blind employee with blindness skills to navigate safely and effectively around a place of employment using either a white cane or guide dog.

The above examples take place at the Seattle Lighthouse every day.

While providing other employers with blueprints on how jobs can be made accessible, the Lighthouse continues to maintain and create job opportunities at the Lighthouse itself. We at the Seattle Lighthouse strive to create opportunities so that blind and Deaf-Blind individuals can lead independent, self-sufficient lives. I am confident that the Lighthouse will remain a place where blind people can find jobs that fit a variety of interests and skill levels, but we can't become complacent. Until blind employees have choices equal to those of sighted persons, our work is incomplete.

A cornerstone of our organization is more than fifty years of collaboration with The Boeing Company, which is outlined in Chapter 5. The Lighthouse is committed to serving this partner by meeting the highest quality and delivery standards. I foresee Boeing and the Seattle Lighthouse continuing to work closely to maintain and expand employment opportunities for blind people in the machining area. Those jobs—operating cutting-edge manufacturing equipment in the production of aircraft parts—are not available for blind people anywhere else in the country.

While developing a successful relationship with Boeing, we also have been building partnerships with the federal government under the Javits-Wagner-O'Day (JWOD) program. I anticipate the creation of high-quality jobs for blind and Deaf-Blind people through our production and distribution of products for federal customers. For instance, we are in the beginning stage of implementing an e-commerce distribution channel for business cards and other custom products for federal employees. As this channel grows, so will the number of high-quality jobs for individuals who are blind. An e-commerce distribution channel is by definition a digital environment, and a blind person can compete on an equal footing in that environment through the use of adaptive technology such as Braille displays and screen-reading software. At the same time, more production jobs will become available for individuals who work in those areas. JWOD also offers opportunities to provide services to military bases, including switchboard jobs.

Technology offers us a grand opportunity to place blind individuals on an equal footing with sighted citizens. Blind people can now access the same information as sighted workers. They can communicate at the same speed and perform thousands of job functions that were previously inaccessible to them. Technology and accessibility considerations have become an integral part of every decision we make concerning new product development and job creation. Furthermore, we are eager to create career paths and give blind employees the training and orientation they need to become supervisors, managers, and executive staff.

The Lighthouse for the Blind is about much more than a place to earn a pay-

Kirk Adams, director of public relations and resource development, reads Braille documents in an office equipped with adaptive technology.

check. It provides employees with whatever training, technology, and services they need to succeed. For one group in particular, our Deaf-Blind employees, these accommodations can become complex and expensive. However, we are committed to maintaining and expanding our Deaf-Blind program. We anticipate increased demand for our unique Deaf-Blind services, especially one-of-a-kind computer training that gives Deaf-Blind people the tools needed to use the Internet and e-mail. Just imagine the doors that will open when a Deaf-Blind person can access the information and communication power of the Internet! As word spreads that Seattle is a place where a Deaf-Blind person can lead a life of independence and self-sufficiency, I am confident that the local Deaf-Blind community will continue to grow.

Essentially, the Lighthouse is about choice—providing blind and Deaf-Blind people with real options. The right to the pursuit of happiness, as our forefathers wrote, must apply to all. We at the Lighthouse want to be part of a community that extends the same range of choices to its blind and Deaf-Blind members as it does to its sighted and hearing citizens.

The Seattle Lighthouse will have been successful when blind teenagers in our community compete equally with their sighted classmates for those first entry-level jobs. It may not be flipping burgers. It may be data entry, operating a telephone switchboard, or doing Internet research. We will celebrate that success when those young blind people take their job experience and education and seek the next highest position. And we'll know our vision has become reality when those same blind individuals have to make tough decisions about which job offer to take.

Until that day arrives for the majority of blind people in our community, we at The Lighthouse for the Blind, Inc., will strive to create more opportunities for independence and self-sufficiency, and continue to seek others who are committed to doing the same.

ACKNOWLEDGMENTS

Seattle Lighthouse trustee Tom Kuebler is one of my lifelong friends. Individuals who are blind or visually impaired are high on Tom's list of interests, in part because his two sons, Jeffrey and Joe, have an inherited and progressive loss of vision called retinitis pigmentosa (RP). I'm grateful to Tom for suggesting my name to the Lighthouse board to be the author of this book. This project opened new vistas for me and, I believe, made me a better person.

Kirk Adams took over Seattle Lighthouse Development and Public Relations in 2000, inaugurating a new millennium and a new Lighthouse mandate. He has been my mentor and touchstone as I waded and floundered toward completion of the book. I must add that Kirk's development team has been helpful and interested in the book project, and they deserve to be mentioned here: Jeff Patterson, Jennifer Moore, Sherry Gomes, and Allison Ryan.

My efforts were expertly guided and assisted by a dedicated "Committee of Six": board members Doug Klan, Ray Haman, and Tom Kuebler; Lighthouse president George "Jake" Jacobson; and key employees Paula Hoffman and Kirk Adams.

Board members Bruce Walker, Fred Mendoza, Oly Wise, Jay Jones, and Ben Woo gave me positive counsel and helpful ideas.

My thanks are also given to a host of Seattle Lighthouse employees and several casual visitors and contractors. Because I had a temporary office within Lighthouse premises, most of those individuals were seen in hallways and workplaces. Our conversations were sometimes brief but always enlightening and interesting.

The following Seattle Lighthouse individuals deserve a longer salute. Most of them took the time to read, criticize, edit, and shape my work. Among the most helpful individuals was former Lighthouse director Rudy Elmer. Director of manufacturing Don Helsel was among the first to offer unqualified cooperation. Quality manager Paul Fletcher made himself available and calmly responded to my wayward queries. Director of engineering services Norm Slader provided books and documents and answered my naïve questions, several of which surely tried his patience. Lighthouse facilities manager Clem Provatakis saw that I had a convenient office, including a chair, desk, and telephone. When I couldn't find an answer anywhere else, Donna Masuda, assistant to Lighthouse president George Jacobson, came up with the information.

Other current and former Lighthouse employees who gave interviews or provided background information are Robert S. "Bob" Johnson, vice president of sales and marketing, who seemed to recall everything about early Lighthouse years. Bob also read and helpfully critiqued the unedited book manuscript. Others were Roosevelt Stevenson, Jenné Arnold, Amy Koehl, Margarita Eng, Lanny Shuman, and Gina Lewis. Hanako "Hank" Nakagawa, assistant to director Rudy Elmer, worked thirty-six years in the blindness field.

Don Donaldson, former principal at the Washington State School for the Blind, in Vancouver, Washington, described how he sold brooms for the Lighthouse in the early 1930s. I also dipped into Don's master's thesis, a history of the Vancouver school. Don's experiences are recounted in his recently published (2004) autobiography, *What's in a Name.*

Development associate Jeff Patterson, drawing on his interest in Seattle Lighthouse history, uncovered valuable caches of records and photos. Bill Boon, internal auditor, did yeoman's service in trying to straighten me out on certification and several Lighthouse money matters. Bruce Keller, director of finance, kept a close watch on contracts and payments related to the project. Bruce also helped find answers to other exotic questions I raised about the Lighthouse.

Seattle Lighthouse friends providing helpful comment include Robert M. Arnold, whose mother, Grace Heffernan (Mrs. Lawrence) Arnold was a Lighthouse board member for many years. Seattle historian James F. Brinkley, Jr., contributed pertinent family details. Susan Backus Stoller and her brother John Backus recalled the dedication of their mother, Mrs. Manson Backus (Frances), as a board member. Governor Albert D. Rosellini resuscitated memories of the Handcrest/

Lighthouse merger, in which he and his staff played key roles. Carolyn (Mrs. William) Danz and Priscilla (Mrs. Harold) Drebin told me about their wonderful mother, Helen Blumenthal, and her many years of working with blind persons.

Volunteer Helen Hauck reminisced about reading to former Lighthouse director Michael Cariola, who was blind. After business was taken care of, Helen recalled that Cariola liked to talk about his Philadelphia roots and visits to Mount Rainier.

Dr. Walter Petersen, an eminent Seattle ophthalmologist and a friend of mine, took time from his busy schedule to research causes and treatment of eye diseases. Board member and ophthalmologist Dr. Robert R. Francis added his expert comment.

An old friend, Bill Nightingale, who was blinded by a farm accident, and his daughter Noel, who has RP, provided interesting and original comment. Likewise New York writer Ved Mehta, who is blind, voiced strong opinions about blindness and institutions that support blind and visually impaired persons.

Jane Powell Thomas, whom I have known most of my life, provided information about her uncle, Handcrest founder Neal Tourtellotte. Thanks to Teresa Summers, who read the early manuscript with a keen eye. Paul Spitzer, former Boeing historian and fellow member of the Pacific Northwest Historians Guild, directed me to Boeing sources. Ken King stepped forward to describe his work for the Lighthouse while he was with the Mitutoyo/MTI Corporation. His efforts centered on developing a "talking device" that could be used with Mitutoyo micrometers, calipers, digital indicators, and digital readouts.

Many individuals from local institutions lent their help. I regret that most of their names have drifted from my poor memory, but the venerable organizations they represent are indelible. I am grateful to the Seattle Public Library, the University of Washington Libraries and the Museum of History & Industry. I also appreciated information from The Washington State Jewish Historical Society. Other sources were the Boeing Company Archives; the Washington Talking Book and Braille Library; the Online Encyclopedia of Seattle and King County, familiarly known as (www.historylink.org); and, of course, The Lighthouse for the Blind, Inc.

Despite the professional and carefully thought-out contributions of many individuals, any errors, omissions, and the occasional author's viewpoint are firmly laid at my door.

Family members have always given me a full measure of encouragement and love. The Lighthouse Project was pleasant and productive in part because of the support of kin: wife Joanne Marie—who is also a no-nonsense editor; daughter Julie; son Steve; and Honeymae, my bright and beautiful granddaughter who likes to read books. Here's another one for her library.

On behalf of The Lighthouse for the Blind, Inc., I tender special thanks to the following individuals who made generous financial contributions to the Book Project:

Kirk Adams
Loren Anderson
Robert M. Arnold
Katherine M. Beck
Herb & Shirley Bridge
Tim Crow
Carolyn Danz
David Davis
Priscilla Drebin
Emil Dupuy
Constance Engelstad
Dr. Robert Francis
Ray Haman
Don Helsel
Paula Hoffman
George Jacobson
Robert S. Johnson
Jens Jorgensen
Karen Kidd

Doug Klan
Bob and Sue Kuebler
Sylvia Kuebler
Tom Kuebler
James Linardos
Carole McBride-Pedersen
Fred Mendoza
Al Mladenich
Don Mollet
Becky Petersen
Dr. Walter Petersen
Brooks Ragen
Henry Robinett
Patrick Sullivan
Teresa Summers
Theresa Szeliga
Bruce Walker
Ken Wherry
Oly Wise

Junius Rochester
Seattle, Washington

Seattle Lighthouse
The Lighthouse for the Blind, Inc.

Seattle Lighthouse for the Blind Foundation

On December 13, 2002, the Seattle Lighthouse for the Blind Foundation was incorporated. Created by the Lighthouse board of trustees, the foundation acts as the organization's fund-raising arm, supporting maintenance and expansion of Lighthouse programs and helping build an endowment fund.

Shortly after incorporation, the foundation received its first substantial gift: $89,448.68 from the estate of Evelyn S. Egtvedt. Mrs. Egtvedt passed away at age 101 on November 19, 2002. Her husband, Clairmont L. Egtvedt, joined The Boeing Company in 1917 as a draftsman and mechanical engineer, later becoming president, general manager, and chairman of the board.

Please contact the Seattle Lighthouse for the Blind Foundation to discuss bequeathing gifts through wills or planned gifts that can provide life income and tax advantages for donors.

For more information, call the director of public relations and resource development at 206 436 2110 or by e-mail at (information@seattlelh.org).

Thank you.

MISSION STATEMENT

To create and enhance opportunities for independence and self-sufficiency of people who are blind, Deaf-Blind, and blind with other disabilities.

How We Do It

We accomplish this by providing employment opportunities, comprehensive vocational, Independent Living and computer training, a wide range of additional support services and outreach/educational programs for external employers and the larger community.

Be Our Guest

We would be delighted to welcome you as our guest at the Seattle Lighthouse so you can learn more about how we are creating opportunities for the independence and self-sufficiency of people who are blind in our community.

Who Should Visit The Seattle Lighthouse?

Employers. If you are interested in making jobs at your workplace accessible for blind applicants, come and see firsthand how it's done.

Financial supporters. We appreciate your generosity and want to show you what you have helped to build. You will be amazed!

Community members. If you are interested in creating opportunities for people who are blind, visit us and learn more about our mission and programs. Let's talk about how we can work together.

We have set aside dates and times throughout the year for public tours. To receive a tour schedule, contact the Seattle Lighthouse at 206 436 2110 or email (information@seattlelh.org).

If you are unable to take a personal tour of the Seattle Lighthouse, you can enjoy a video tour by contacting the Development Office at 206 436 2110. Two free six-minute professionally produced videotapes will be sent to you. Both videotapes are also available on a single CD-ROM.

Useful Lighthouse Web sites include:
www.deafblindlh.org
www.seattlelighthouse.org
www.lighthousestore.org

BIBLIOGRAPHY
Books

Anonymous. *History of the Lighthouse for the Blind, Inc.* Seattle
(?): no publisher, 1990 (10 pages).

Cornish, Nellie C. *Miss Aunt Nellie: The Autobiography of
Nellie C. Cornish.* Seattle: University of Washington
Press, 1964

Dickman, Irving R. *Creating Jobs: Changing Lives: The
Wagner-O'Day Act and the Workshops for the Blind.* New
York: National Industries for the Blind, 1989 (?).

Dixon, Judith M., ed. *Braille into the Next Millennium.*
Washington, D.C.: National Library Service for the
Blind and Physically Handicapped, 2000.

Donaldson, Don. *A History of the Washington State School for
the Blind.* Seattle: University of Washington, 1938 (a
thesis submitted for the degree of master of arts).

—*What's in a Name.* Bloomington, Ind.: 1st Books, 2004.

Edman, Polly K. *Tactile Graphics.* New York: AFB Press,
1992.

Eaton, Allen H. *Beauty for the Sighted and the Blind.* New
York: St. Martin's Press, 1959 (foreword by Helen
Keller).

Esterman, Ben. *The Eye Book.* Arlington, Va.: Great
Ocean Publishers, 1977.

Ficken, Robert E. *Washington Territory*. Pullman, Wash.: WSU Press, 2002.

Freedman, Russell. *Out of Darkness: The Story of Louis Braille*. New York: Clarion Books, 1997.

Haley, Delphine. *Dorothy Stimson Bullitt*. Seattle: Sasquatch Books, 1995.

Halliwell, Leslie. *Halliwell's Filmgoer's Companion*. New York: Charles Scribner's Sons, 1988

Hermann, Dorothy. *Helen Keller: A Life*. New York: Alfred A. Knopf, 1998.

Hickok, Lorena A. *The Story of Helen Keller*. New York: Grosset & Dunlap, 1958.

Jepson, Jill, ed. *No Walls of Stone*. Washington, D.C.: Gallaudet University Press, 2002.

Kendrick, Deborah. *Jobs to be Proud of: Profiles of Workers Who Are Blind or Visually Impaired*. New York: AFB Press, 1993.

LeFevre, Robert. *The Story of the Wagner-O'Day Act*. New York: National Industries for the Blind, 1966.

Majeska, Marilyn Lundell. *Talking Books: Pioneering and Beyond*. Washington, D.C.: National Library Service for the Blind and Physically Handicapped, 1988.

Meany, Edmond S. *History of the State of Washington*. New York: The Macmillan Co., 1950.

Moulton, Gary E., ed. *The Lewis and Clark Journals*. Lincoln, Neb., and London: University of Nebraska Press, 2003.

Norden, Martin F. *The Cinema of Isolation*. New Brunswick, N.J.: Rutgers University Press, 1994.

Paciorek, Michael J., and Jeffery A. Jones. *Sports and Recreation for the Disabled: A Resource Manual*. Indianapolis, Ind.: Benchmark Press, Inc., 1989.

Rochester, Junius. *The Last Electric Trolley: Madrona &
Denny-Blaine, Seattle, Washington Neighborhoods.* Seattle:
Tommie Press, 2002.

Serling, Robert J. *Legend and Legacy: The Story of Boeing and
Its People.* New York: St. Martin's Press, 1992.

Smith, Jean Kennedy, and George Plimpton. *Chronicles of
Courage: Very Special Artists.* New York: Random House,
1993.

Other Sources

Elmer, Rudolph E. Personal files, Issaquah, Wash.,
1950s–1970s

Handcrest, Inc. General files held at The Lighthouse for
the Blind, Inc. Seattle, 1950s–1960s.

HistoryLink (www.historylink.org). Online Metropedia
for Seattle and King County. Seattle, 2004.

Horizons. Newsletters of The Lighthouse for Blind, Inc.
Seattle, 2000–2003.

Insight. Newsletters of The Lighthouse for the Blind, Inc.
Seattle, 1990s.

Fresh Sheet. Quarterly bulletin of The Lighthouse for the
Blind, Inc. Seattle, 1990s.

Lighthouse for the Blind, Inc., The. Files. Seattle,
1920s–1990s.

Museum of History & Industry. Archives. Seattle,
1960s–1980s.

National Industries for the Blind. Annual reports. New
York, 1980s–1990s.

Newsletter. A publication of The Lighthouse for the Blind,
Inc. Seattle, April–June, 1990.

Newspapers: *Seattle Mail & Herald, Seattle Times, Seattle Post-Intelligencer*, 1906–1993. On microfilm at the Seattle Public Library.

Opportunity. Publication of the National Industries for The Blind. Bloomfield, N.J., April/May 1981.

PACCAR World. Magazine for PACCAR employees. Bellevue, Wash., September 1978.

Puget Soundings. Newsletter of the Fleet and Industrial Supply Center. Puget Sound, Wash., May/June 1996.

University of Washington, University Archives and Manuscripts Division. Several papers. Seattle, 1980s.

INDEX

AUTHOR BIO

JUNIUS ROCHESTER is a third-generation native of the Pacific Northwest. He attended Seattle's Garfield High School; Whitman College, Walla Walla, Washington; and the Harvard Business School, Boston, Massachusetts.

He is the author of five books, numerous articles, and was regional historian/narrator at KUOW-FM, Seattle's outlet for National Public Radio. In 1995, Junius was given a Project Award by the Association of King County Historical Organizations and the King County Landmarks and Heritage Commission.

Junius gives talks on Pacific Northwest topics and is frequently a guest historian aboard cruise ships. He is past president of the Pacific Northwest Historians Guild, an officer in the Pioneer Association of the State of Washington, and holds membership in the Washington State Historical Society, the Oregon Historical Society, the Alaska Historical Society, and the Lewis and Clark Trail Heritage Foundation, Inc.

Seattle Lighthouse

Seattle Lighthouse for the Blind
F O U N D A T I O N

December 13, 2007

Dear Roger and Shirley,

As we enter into a new year, I wanted to take this opportunity to thank you for your commitment to providing opportunities for independence to blind and Deaf-Blind adults in our community. Your support has allowed the Lighthouse to expand our services and reach more blind and Deaf-Blind individuals in need of employment, training, and support services.

Please accept this complimentary copy of our Lighthouse history book *Seattle's Best Kept Secret*. This book was funded by the Lighthouse Board of Directors and highlights the growth and development of the Seattle Lighthouse throughout its 90 year history.

As a key supporter of the Lighthouse, you are a part of our continuing evolution

blind with other disabilities. On behalf of all of us here, thank you again and we hope you enjoy the book. Best wishes to you and your loved ones in 2008!

Sincerely,

President-elect
Seattle Lighthouse for the Blind